The Beginner's Guide to Financial Spread Betting

Step-by-step instructions and winning strategies

By Michelle Baltazar

HARRIMAN HOUSE LTD

3A Penns Road
Petersfield
Hampshire
GU32 2EW
GREAT BRITAIN

Tel: +44 (0)1730 233870
Fax: +44 (0)1730 233880
Email: enquiries@harriman-house.com
Website: www.harriman-house.com

First published in Great Britain in 2005, this 2nd edition published in 2008
Copyright © Harriman House Ltd

The right of Michelle Baltazar to be identified as the author has been
asserted
in accordance with the Copyright, Design and Patents Act 1988.

ISBN: 1-905641-82-6
ISBN 13: 978-1-905641-82-6

British Library Cataloguing in Publication Data
A CIP catalogue record for this book can be obtained from the British
Library.

Printed and bound by CPI Antony Rowe, Chippenham and Eastbourne.

Contents

Biography

Michelle Baltazar is an award-winning finance journalist. She wrote a weekly column on derivatives for London-based investment magazine *Shares*. Prior to *Shares*, she worked for Australian business magazine, *Business Review Weekly*.

Acknowledgements

I would like to thank everyone at ETX Capital for their support and input, with special thanks to Andrew Edwards, Alex Sawyer and Mic Mills.

I am also grateful to everyone from the spread betting and CFD industry who have taken the time to do the interviews for this book. Special mention goes to Dominic Connolly, David Buik and Jim Morrison. While at *Shares*, they helped me gain insight on how the world of derivatives trading works.

My publisher Philip Jenks deserves a special mention for his hand in transforming this book from a two-page idea to the finished product it is now. Nick Read, also from Harriman House, made sure all the i's were dotted and the t's were crossed.

On a more personal note, thanks to everyone I worked with at *Shares* and to the three people who 'took a bet' on me: Ross Greenwood, Narelle Hooper and Ali Cromie.

Finally, to my family and friends: *thank you*.

Introduction

In the summer of 2003, two close friends from south-east London, Clive Smith*, an owner of a travel agency, and Joan Irving*, a school teacher, made a decision that would soon change their lives.

They placed a bet of £1,000 on a handful of shares through a form of trading called spread betting. The pair traded a host of shares including online company MyTravel, airline giant British Airways and pharmaceuticals group SkyePharma.

Eight weeks later, that £1,000 turned to winnings of more than £1 million.

You would be hard pressed to find any other form of trading that allows such a scale of return possible for the average punter. Spread betting was once the domain of institutional investors, City traders and high rollers. Not anymore. Clive Smith and Joan Irving are just two of more than 100,000 people across the country that have turned to it as a natural extension to their investment strategies.

In between turning £1,000 to £1 million, there were periods where the bet could have gone either way. To make the chain of decisions they had made, involved more than luck and sheer guts. They did their research, attended shareholder meetings and kept abreast with market news.

The aim of this book is to give you a basic understanding of how spread betting works, so that, just like Smith and Irving, you can find out how to turn a pauper's budget into a king's ransom.

It is worth noting that before they made their million, Smith and Irving made some costly mistakes. This brings us to an issue that should be at the forefront of a novice spread better's mind: managing risk. The secondary aim of this book is to explain the risks involved, and how to reduce them.

---

* Details have been changed.

The road to successful spread betting starts with education. By the time you finish reading this book, you should know how to place a spread bet, the rules of the game and how to trade successfully. The appendices and glossary at the back serve as your quick and handy cheat notes when you start trading. As the saying goes: 'Don't just learn the tricks of the trade. Learn the trade.'

1

Why spread bet?

"Progress always involves risk; you can't steal second base and keep your foot on first."

– **Frederick Wilcox, author**

What is spread betting?

Let's start with a question.

If you have £1,000 of spare savings, and you want to invest in the stock market, what is the best way to do it?

If you have the time and the inclination to research companies, you could buy shares directly in a handful of companies and manage your investments yourself.

If you don't have confidence in your own stock-picking abilities, you could buy units in a unit trust or other collective fund. A fund manager would then make decisions about which companies your money is invested in and take a fee for his service.

If you don't fancy paying the costs for professional advice, you could put your £1,000 into an index or tracker fund. This would diversify your investment across a wide range of companies and ensure that you get the same return as the market average, no better, no worse.

All these options are valid. None are inherently better than the others. Their suitability depends on your personal circumstances.

However, there is another option which will, potentially, allow you to make much higher returns from your £1,000. It is called spread betting.

Spread betting is a form of trading in which you bet on the price movement of a share, index, currency, commodity or bond. It is a way of playing the stock markets without actually owning any shares.

The concept was created in the 1970s by a then 35-year old investment banker called Stuart Wheeler. But it is only since the late 1990s that spread betting has gained widespread appeal. **In a nutshell, it allows access to markets that were previously restricted to institutions, banks and wealthy investors.**

How? The three main catalysts are the internet, the increased volatility in world markets and the simplicity of spread betting.

- The **internet** jump-started enormous changes to the workings of the stock market. First, it allows easy access to market information that traditionally was only available to institutions and wealthy investors. Second, it allows investors to try their hands at investing 'anonymously'. Third, online trading systems have lowered charges to a level that is practical for both the average investor and the spread betting company.

- The recent subprime crisis in the US, which carried across into the European markets, sent the stock markets tumbling. Spread betting was an ideal medium to take advantage of these markets, as unlike conventional share trading it **allows investors to bet on markets going down.** The falling markets provided plenty of these so-called 'short-selling' opportunities. We will cover this more fully in chapter 8.

- **Simplicity.** Spread betting is a type of derivative (a financial instrument that is 'derived' from an underlying market such as equities). Of all the derivatives available, it is seen as the easiest to understand.

From one product (the gold price) in the 1970s, there are now more than 4,000 financial and non-financial instruments to choose from. Financial instruments include equities, commodities and indices, while non-financial ones include sports and fancy bets.

In short, the industry is continually changing shape to reach a wider market.

Pros

The main advantages of spread betting, all of which are explained more fully later in this book, are:

- It is **easier to understand** than other financial instruments. The process is less complex than that for options, futures and Contracts for Difference (CFDs).

- You can start with a **small amount of capital**. You can open an account for less than £100. Trades can be placed from an account balance as low as £28.

- You only **pay a fraction of the full cost of the trade,** usually 10%, up front. This is called **margin trading.**

- It enables you to profit from rising (bull) or falling (bear) markets.

- It is **commission-free.** All the costs associated with the bet are built into the bid-offer spread.

- Gains are not taxable. Unlike share trading where gains made are potentially taxed at your current income tax rate, spread bets are not subject to capital gains tax.

- There are also income tax savings. For example, if you own a share paying a dividend, **income from that dividend is taxable at your current income tax rate**. Spread bets do not pay dividends. Instead, the dividend payment is built into the price so the holder of a position in a dividend-paying share will reap the rewards in the form of a cheaper buy price.

- No **stamp duty**. Spread bets are free from stamp duty, currently charged at 0.5% on all share purchases. This is because a spread bet is a contract between the client and the spread betting company and no physical exchange of shares actually takes place.

- The savings do add up. For a purchase of £5,000 of any share, the stamp duty charge paid to the government is £25. A trader who deals twice a week, 52 weeks a year will end up paying £2,600 in stamp duties alone.

- If you were to trade £25,000 in normal share transactions each trading day via a stockbroker, you would pay the government more than £31,500 in stamp duty over a year.

Other advantages:

- **One account** for a range of financial products. One spread betting account allows investors to trade indices, single shares, currencies, commodities, bonds and options on a number of global markets.

- **Instant execution.** Spread betting companies are not brokers, so all trades placed are contracts between the client and the spread betting company. This means that each execution is not necessarily traded over an exchange so there is no delay in routing the order. This allows instant execution in markets where this would not normally be possible.

- **No currency risk.** Dealing in foreign shares can be cumbersome and impractical if you are an average investor. You have to deal with a third party and pay transaction charges. **Spread betting allows traders to bet in pounds per point on international shares.**

- **Dealing in pounds per point,** dollars per point or euros per point makes tracking your investments much easier. For example, if share X is up 15 points on the day, it is far easier to estimate your profit by calculating that you have made, say, a £125 per point increase than calculating your number of shares, say 12,500 multiplied by 15 points, less broker charges stamp duty, tax and so on.

- **Extended trading hours.** Some spread betting companies are open 24 hours a day. This is in contrast to normal market trading hours, which run from 7.00am to 9.00pm.

- **Less paperwork** is involved compared to conventional share dealing.

- Setting up a spread betting account is simple and easy. All that is required, in most cases, is a signed application form and utility bill.

- It is a **practical form of short-term investing** to complement any long-term investments.

- Trades executed online are **anonymous, fast and cheap**.

- **Online trading platforms** for spread betting are said to be more advanced compared to those for traditional share dealing.

- Some spread betting companies offer a **virtual trading platform** for you to practice on. This offers an opportunity for potential spread betters to understand the markets, the dealing process and test trading strategies before committing real money. The ability to practice with virtual money reduces the risk of entering into incorrect positions and helps novice traders to understand the risks involved in dealing with geared products.

- Spread betting companies provide access to investment research, news, tutorials, market updates and commentary that are normally only available to institutions.

- The **type of bets** you can do range from financial (shares, indices, commodities, currencies), sports-based (football, horse racing, rugby) to fanciful (how many sips of water the Chancellor is going to drink during his Budget speech).

- **Unlimited profits with limited losses.** You can control when you want to take profits and run your bet until the point at which you decide to close it. The losses can be unlimited too but, as we shall discover later, they can be capped through stop-losses.

Cons

The disadvantages are:

- **You incur your loss when you close the trade** (all spread bets have an expiry date). With conventional share dealing, you crystallise your loss only when you sell the shares (no expiry date).

- If spread betting on equities, **you do not get dividends** because you are betting on a price movement rather than buying the shares. You get the benefit of the dividend through the price.

- The spread is different to the cash market spread so you have to factor in a certain increase or decrease in the price before you are in profit.

- Losses on bets **cannot be offset against capital gains** you make either on other spread bets or from your conventional share investments.

- You can lose more than your initial deposit or capital. The margin trading involved means that while potential profits are magnified, potential losses are also magnified, except for trades with stop losses. With ordinary share trading, you cannot lose more than the amount you invested in the shares. With spread betting, there is no such limit.

- Spread betting is not ideal for long-term investing as costs are incurred each time a spread bet is 'rolled' over or extended to a new expiry date. All spread bets have a definite expiry date. If you wish to run your trade beyond the expiry date you must roll your position over from one quarter to the next.

Key points

- Spread betting allows access to markets that were previously restricted to institutions, banks and wealthy investors.

- There are pros and cons to spread betting. Profits are not taxable. However, in spread betting you can lose more than your initial capital.

- The industry is continually changing shape to appeal to a wider market.

How it works

"You can't stop the waves, but you can learn to surf"

– Jon Kabat-Zinn, meditation expert

The basics

Using shares as an example, the basic steps are:

Step 1: You ask for a bid-offer quote from a spread betting company.

Step 2: If you think the shares are going to rise above the offer price, you buy.

If you think the shares are going to fall below the bid price, you sell.

Step 3: You tell them the size of the stake you want to bet, say £1 or £10, per point movement of the price.

Step 4: You tell them the total funds you wish to risk and place an appropriate stop-loss.

That's it.

Illustration 2.1 – Main components of a spread bet

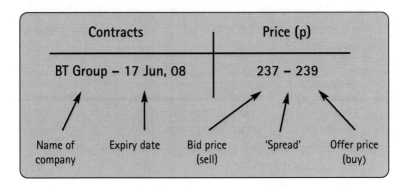

What you need to know

- In the previous illustration, a spread betting company gives a two-way quote 237 – 239 (in pound and penny by default i.e. £2.37 – £2.39), offering you the choice to either buy or sell BT shares.

- The higher or 'offer' price is for buyers and the lower or 'bid' price is for sellers. If you think the price of BT shares will rise above the offer price of 239p before the expiry date (17 Jun 08) is reached, you buy (also known as an **'up bet'** or **'going long'**).

- Conversely, if you think the price of BT shares will fall below the bid price of 237p before the expiry date is reached, you sell (also known as a **'down bet'** or **'going short'**).

- You specify how much in pounds (£), dollars ($) or euros (€) you wish to bet (called the **'stake'**) per point movement (or per **'tic'**) in BT. In this case, one point or one tic is equivalent to a penny movement in BT shares.

- **The expiry date** is the date when the bet is closed and you settle any profits or losses. However, **you can close the bet anytime** before the expiry date (as long as it is within the quoted market hours for that product). You can also roll it over to the next expiry date.

- As you are trading on a 'per point' movement of the shares either way, there is no **fixed amount** that you can win or lose. Your profits (or losses) are equivalent to a multiple of your stake. For example, if BT shares rise 5 points from 239p to 244p before the expiry date is reached, you win £50 on a £10 stake per point bet (£10 x 5 points = £50).

- As you are betting on the price movement only, **you do not own the underlying share at any point**.

A typical conversation

For easy reading, trading examples throughout this book will feature two fictitious characters: **John**, the average trader and *Mark*, the dealer from fictitious spread betting company **Spreadco**.

While spread betting can be applied to many financial products such as indices, equities, currencies and commodities, most of the examples in this book will refer to shares. The mechanics of the bet are the same across all products.

Opening a trade

Dialogue 1. How to open a trade

John thinks the shares of Lloyds are going to go up, so he places a buy bet at 435. A typical conversation will go like this:

Mark: Good afternoon, Spreadco group, Mark speaking. Can I help you?

John: Can I have a price in June Lloyds please?

Mark: June Lloyds is 451 – 455, sir.

John: I would like to buy £10 at 455 please.

Mark: Is that to open or close, sir?

John: To open.

Mark: Asks for John's account number and checks if he has sufficient funds in account. Sir, you buy £10 of June Lloyds at 455 to open.

John: (May confirm trade again.)

Mark: (Would then put trade in system.)

What you need to know

1. John asked for 'June Lloyds' meaning he wanted the spread betting company's bid-offer quote for the shares of Lloyds Bank.

2. June is the month of the quarterly expiry date at which John's bet will 'expire'. The expiry date is the Tuesday before the third Wednesday of the quarterly months March, June, September and December. **John can close the bet on, or anytime before, this expiry date. If he does not close the bet before expiry or give instructions to roll the bet over to the next expiry period, the bet will automatically close on the expiry date.**

3. The quote 451 – 455 means John can place a sell bet at 451, if he thinks Lloyds shares will fall below this level in the future, or he can place a buy bet at 455, if he thinks Lloyds shares will rise above this level in the future.

4. 'Buy £10 at 455' means John is placing a £10 bet per one point movement or '**tic**' of the shares.

5. '**Is that to open or close?**' This is Mark asking John whether he wants to start a new bet (to open) or he wants to settle an existing bet (to close).

6. **The act of opening and closing bets differentiates spread betting from conventional share trading.** In spread betting, you close a bet by calling up the spread betting company and making a contra or opposite bet. For example, if John called to make an up bet, he can only close that bet by making a down bet (contra bet) for exactly the same amount. In other words, John puts in two bets, the first bet to open and the second to close in order to settle one trade.

7. 'To open'. In this case, John is opening a bet.

8. (Checks to see if John has enough funds.) In spread betting, you do not have to pay the full cost of the trade. This is called margin trading. However, you do need to have a certain amount of money in your account to draw against that trade. This is called the **Notional Trading Requirement** (NTR) and is explained later in this chapter.

Closing a trade

Three days later, the share price of Lloyds goes up to 458p and John decides to take profits.

Dialogue 2: How to close a trade

Mark: (Spread bet company.) Good afternoon, Spreadco, Mark speaking. Can I help you?

John: Can I have a price in June Lloyds please?

Mark: Dec Lloyds is 458 – 462 sir.

John: I would like to sell £10 at 458 please.

Mark: Is that to open or close, sir?

John: To close.

Mark: (Takes John's account number.) Sir, you sell £10 of Dec Lloyds at 458 to close.

John: (May confirm trade again.)

Mark: (Would then put trade in system.)

What you need to know

- As discussed earlier, **you close a bet by placing a 'contra' bet** or an opposite bet. In this case, John called to sell £10 at 458p as an opposite bet to his £10 buy bet three days ago.

- His profit is a multiple of his per point bet. 458 – 465 = 3 points increase. £10 x 3 = £30 profit.

Margin requirements

In spread betting, you do not have to pay the full cost of the bet up front. However, you do need to have sufficient funds in your account to cover any potential losses – usually called the Notional Trading Requirement (NTR) – although terms may vary.

The NTR is calculated in two ways:

1. 10% of the actual value of your maximum potential loss on a trade

---

Dialogue 3: Calculating the deposit required

John: Hi Mark, I'd like to place a £1 buy bet on Lloyds. How much margin do I have to place on that?

Mark: Well John, your maximum potential loss would occur if Lloyds shares fall from 455p to zero. That is, £1 x 455 points = £455. Placing a £1 bet on a share that trades at 455p requires a 10% margin on your maximum potential loss. That's £45.50.

John: I see, that means I have to put in £45.50 to make the bet? Thanks Mark.

Mark: You're welcome.

---

2. As a multiple of a pre-determined value called the 'bet size factor' (again, the term may vary)

Dialogue 4: What is a bet size factor?

John: Hi Mark, I just spoke to someone who said that instead of the 10% margin rule, some spread betting companies also quote a bet size factor. Is that true?

Mark: Yes. It's basically the same principle.

John: So if I want to place a £1 buy bet on the Wall Street June contract, how much do I have to put in as margin?

Mark: The range of bet size factors for different products are listed either on the company's website or given to you when you apply for an account. With the Wall Street December contract, the bet size factor is 500. That means your NTR is £500.

John: I see. Can you get me a copy of this bet size factors table?

Mark: I can, but you trade online and the bet size factor list is on the website. Plus, when you trade via the internet, the margin required is automatically calculated for you.

John: Oh yes, I can see it here. But just to be sure, can you email me instructions on how to get to the section that explains bet size factors.

Mark: Sure. You should get the email in the next few minutes.

What you need to know

- Every trade you make will require a separate Notional Trading Requirement (NTR) or initial margin available in your account.

- For example, if you want to place two bets and each requires an NTR of £1,000 then you would need to have £2,000 available in your account before your spread betting company accepts both bets.

- The bet size factor (it may be called something else but the principle is the same) varies according to the volatility of the underlying product. There are various definitions for volatility. In this instance, it is defined as the statistical measure of how much the price of a certain share or asset will move at a certain time or over a certain period of time. **The more volatile a share or an index is, the bigger the bet size factor.**

- When trading online, you do not have to calculate the NTR for each trade as this is done for you. While the format varies between different spread betting companies, the ETX Capital format is as below:

Illustration 2.2 – Example of a trade indicating the margin required

Order Number	Action	Type	Price	Order Amount	Total Funding Available	Required Margin
#722172	Buy	Barclays Plc –17 Jun, 08	488	1	4469.00	41.00

1. £41.00 in margin was reserved on your account for this trade.

2. Your current aggregate position for Barclays Plc – 17 Jun, 08 is 1 Long.

3. You still have £4,469.00 available funds in addition to your total margin reserved. To see your Total Account Value, please click on the Portfolio Manager button.

4. Please note the order number and the trade details for your records.

Margin call

While your bet is open, you will incur what is called an **open profit or loss position**. This is your calculated profit or loss on the bet depending on whether the market is moving in your favour or not. To state the obvious, it only becomes a realised profit or loss when you close the trade.

When you are in an open profit position, you don't have to worry about margin calls. **But when you have an open loss position, the total funds that have to be available from your account will increase.**

If you do not have enough funds in your account then this will result in a 'margin call'. That is, your spread betting services provider will contact you to top up your account.

Illustration 2.3 – When does a margin call happen?

John's cash balance: £1,000

Credit allocation: £0 ← Depending on your account type, deposit or credit. This example is that of a deposit account.

Required Margin (NTR): £500

Open P/L (Profit/Loss): -£250

Total funding available: £250

[£1,000 - £500 (NTR) – £250 open loss]

However, if John's open loss widens to -£600

Total funding available: £100 owing

[£1,000 - £500 (NTR) – £600 open loss]

Mark would then contact John to request more funds. This is called a **margin call**.

Dialogue 5: The margin call

Mark: Hi John, it's Mark from Spreadco* here.

John: Oh yes, is there something wrong?

Mark: No. But I'm calling to tell you that your open loss has exceeded the amount of funds available from your account. With your current open loss of £600, you need to deposit £100 into your account.

John: But it's an 'open loss'. I haven't actually settled the trade. I can already see the price moving up now.

Mark: Yes, but this is one of the differences between conventional share trading and margin trading. With margin trading, you are only required to put in a deposit of the total cost of the trade. But, as a precautionary measure, you have to have a certain level of funds available in your account in case the bet goes against you. It is one way of managing your risk.

John: Hmm, makes sense. It does mean I am more aware when a bet is not doing too well. How much time do I have to put up the extra margin?

Mark: It varies on the size of the bet, who you trade with and your relationship with us. In this case, you get three days. But John, you also have another option. You can reduce your position so you stay within your margin call.

John: Perhaps, reduce it to a £1 bet per point instead of a £2 bet per point?

Mark: Yes.

John: That's good to know. I want to keep it at £2 bet per point so I'll transfer some money online now.

Mark: Thanks, I've just emailed you our bank account details in case you don't have it handy.

John: Wait, what happens if my open loss turns into an open profit?

Mark: You can either keep the extra funds in your account or we give it back to you.

---

* As a policy, if you do not take the call, your spread betting company will not leave a message on your voice mail or with someone disclosing where they are from. They would usually leave their contact number and name, but not the name of the spread betting company they work for.

What you need to know about margin calls

1. Scenario 1: Your spread betting company calls you and requests that you put an additional £100 into your account to cover your open loss. By law, you must meet the margin call within five days. However, the policy differs between spread betting companies (Spreadco's policy is three days). Some companies expect you to meet the margin call immediately. They will try and reach you by phone, email, fax or any other means. **Check the terms and conditions of a spread betting company as it will include an explanation on how to deal with margin calls and how soon you need to pay by.**

At spread betting company City Index, if margin payments are not received in full within three business days of a margin call being made, they may, without telling you, close any or all of your open positions. Margin payments of more than £10,000 may be required by electronic method for same day transfer.

Payments can be made by cheque, electronic banking, debit or credit card.

 Note: It is your responsibility, not your company's, to monitor your positions.

2. Scenario 2: Margin calls don't have to be paid. You can reduce your position to stay within your Notional Trading Requirement.

3. Scenario 3: What everyone wants to avoid is closing out positions forcibly. The treatment of margin calls will depend on how well your spread betting company knows you, your relationship with them and the type of trade you are executing. At spread betting company IG Index, you must be able to meet the call within the same day.

What happens if the price moves back into your favour?

You can either choose for the extra funds to be returned to you or the money stays in your account. Some spread betting services pay you interest on money sitting in your account.

Getting started

Opening a spread betting account is similar to opening a bank account. You provide your chosen spread betting company with your personal details such as name, address, contact number, employment and banking details.

Processing your application form can take 24 hours or more. Your spread betting company will want to check your credit history and double-check the information you gave them.

Some spread betting companies, however, may allow you to start trading before the verification process. This happens if you are going to use a cash account (as opposed to a credit account), or if you are looking at starting with a small amount of capital, e.g. £100.

Either way, a one or two day difference is inconsequential compared to other criteria by which you are going to choose your company from.

While you are waiting for your account to be set up, you can start practising with 'play' money using trading simulators. For example, ETX Capital (⌨ www.ETXCapital.com) offers a virtual trading platform option which allows you to trade a fantasy portfolio worth up to £20,000 using real financial instruments and real prices. This is a very effective way of familiarising yourself with spread betting before committing real money.

What can you spread bet on?

- Stock indices (FTSE, DAX, DOW, CAC, S&P)

- Single shares (US, UK, European)

- Commodities (gold, silver, oil)

- Bonds (Bund, Gilt, BOBL, 10 year note)

- Other products (property prices, weather, interest rates)

- Special interests (how many sips of water the Chancellor will drink while announcing the Budget)

- Sports

In most cases, there are two prices quoted for each product:

- **Daily or intra day bets** – for bets that expire at the end of the day. Again, you can close this anytime before the day ends or roll it over to another day.

- **Quarterly bets** – for bets that expire at the next quarterly expiry date. Again, you can close this anytime before the date or roll it over to the next quarterly date.

Illustration 2.4 – Daily versus quarterly bets

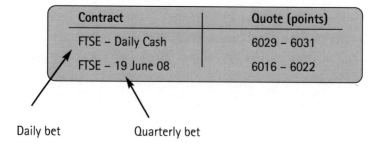

Contract	Quote (points)
FTSE – Daily Cash	6029 – 6031
FTSE – 19 June 08	6016 – 6022

Daily bet   Quarterly bet

What you need to know

- Some spread betting companies offer a hybrid of daily and quarterly bets. For example, you can trade on **weekly bets**. Some companies offer a 'rolling cash bet,' which allows you to keep a bet open for as long as you wish, subject to paying the financing costs associated with it.

- The list of products you can spread bet on continues to grow due to client feedback and requests. If in doubt, check with your spread betting company.

What does a dealing room look like?

The dealing room conforms to the Hollywood stereotype: Lots of people in an open-plan office glued to their trading screens. The mood is frantic from 7am to 8.30am, especially at 8am when the UK and European stock markets open. Trading volumes slow down after the first two hours of the day and can stay quiet until about 1.30pm, when US figures are released. The atmosphere peaks at 2.30pm when the US stock market opens.

Trading stays hectic until about 4.30pm, with trading volumes sometimes picking up at night during US trading hours. It depends on the news flow that filters through the day. The number of economic reports, company results and company news that are due on that day call the tune.

As a client, you can use this information to your benefit in terms of when to contact your services provider and when prices are likely to gyrate wildly. During the busy periods, expect phone calls with your account manager to be brief and, if the market is moving fast, you might get two different quotes in half a breath.

However, the time issue is not a valid excuse to be rude, so if you believe that phone calls either to open or close a trade are unfairly abrupt, chances are there is another spread betting company out there that can offer you better customer service.

Increasingly, **trades are done online**. Some traders prefer to do large bets on the phone.

Is spread betting for me?

Your financial situation, risk tolerance and general investment knowledge determine whether spread betting is right for you.

Be in no doubt, spread betting, like all other forms of trading, is risky and speculative. **Do not bet money that you cannot afford to lose.** Note that not everyone is suited for trading as, arguably, it takes a certain mindset and bravado to deal with the wins, **and** the losses.

Others find trading addictive and, while being passionate in whatever you are doing is a necessary ingredient for success, you have to keep yourself in check. Are you doing it to supplement your income or for the sake of it?

The risk you take should be proportional to your spread betting and trading experience. The advantage of spread betting over other forms of trading is that you can start with relatively small amounts of money. Stakes range from as little as 1p per point movement up to £1,000 per point. If you are a novice, you may want to start with a fantasy trading portfolio.

Be realistic about the amount of time you are willing to commit. If you can only track one trade at a time (also called a **position**) then do just that. Opening several positions without a tracking system in place and the time to monitor them has caught out novices.

You do not need city experience to trade successfully. In a client survey conducted by ETX Capital in March 2007, they found that only 8% of their clients had jobs in finance. Contrary to expectations, the most common profession is in information technology at 22%. Second on the list are the self-employed at 17%.

As for how much they earn in their regular jobs, 42% have an annual salary of between £31,000 and £60,000. Only 24% can be classified as high-income earners (more than £60,000).

What do these numbers mean? They prove that spread betting is not just for the high rollers or City types. Again, the overriding factors are your finances, your risk tolerance, and your general investment knowledge.

Key points

- A spread betting company gives a two way quote. The higher or offer price is for buyers and the lower or bid price is for sellers.

- As you are betting on the price movement only, you do not own the underlying asset at any point.

- You close a bet by placing an opposite or contra bet.

Trading online – a step-by-step guide

"What we have to learn to do, we learn by doing"

– Aristotle, Greek philosopher

This chapter consists of screen shots that will walk you through the different stages of a spread bet. There are references to the chapters that are relevant at each point.

You will also learn how to roll over a trade and the different types of order you can place with your spread betting company.

 Note: You can place a number of orders or a set of instructions with your spread betting company which become a trade when executed.

Opening and closing a trade

Step 1. Opening and closing a trade

(See chapter 2: How it works)

Figure 1. After you log in, you can choose which markets you would like to trade on. The first markets tab (see tabs running along the top) shows the major stock indices such as the FTSE and the S&P.

You can also place spread bets on commodities, currencies, bonds and single shares in the UK, the US and Europe.

Step 2. Placing your order

(See chapter 2: How it works)

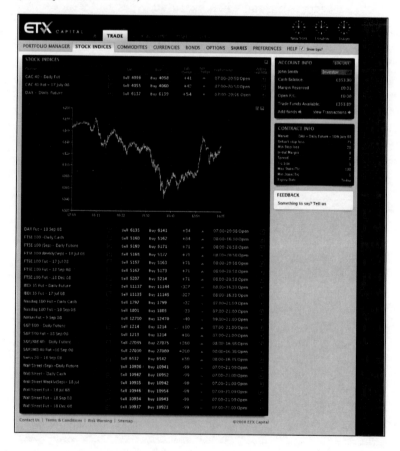

Figure 2. If you want to place a spread bet on the DAX Daily Future, a screen similar to the one above would appear. Details are set in a table in the deal ticket.

Types of orders

What you need to know

You need to learn your VWAPs from your MOOs and your OCOs. These are the types of orders you can make in spread betting. Note that you can have several orders running which are executed as trades as and when they meet your specifications.

Example

Share XYZ is trading at 359 / 362:

1. **Market order** – this is an order to buy or sell at the current price. E.g. buy £10 per point at 362p is a market order.

2. **Limit order** – this is an order to buy or sell at a limit price. This limit price is normally to buy below or sell above the current price, e.g. buy £10 per point at 360p is a limit order that will be filled (executed) if the offer price drops down to 360p.

3. **Stop-loss order** – this is an order to sell if the market falls to a certain level (long client) or buy if the market climbs up to a certain level (short client). Stop-loss orders are combined with an open position to stop out the client should the position move unfavourably. If a trader buys £10 per point at 362p, he or she may leave a stop-loss order to sell at 340p to close out the position should the price fall.

4. **Stop to open order** (momentum order) – this is an order to buy if the market gets up to a certain level or sell if it drops down to a certain level. Unlike a stop-loss order that closes out an open position, a stop to open is designed to open a position if the market is moving in a certain direction. These orders are used by

momentum traders who believe the time to buy is when the market is moving up or sell when the market is moving down. An order to buy £10 per point at 370p to open a new trade is called a 'buy stop'.

5. **GTC** (Good Till Cancelled) – an ongoing order (as opposed to an ongoing trade) until the client calls to cancel it.

6. **GFD** (Good For the Day) – cancelled at the end of the trading day in question.

7. **MOC** (Market on Close) – to be executed at best on the close.

8. **MOO** (Market on Open) – to be executed at best on the open.

9. **OCO** (One Cancels the Other) – two orders are left but the first one to be executed cancels the other

10. **Fill or Kill** – for larger orders, the broker is instructed to get a price for the whole order and depending on the price, fill the whole order or cancel it.

11. **VWAP** (Volume Weighted Average Price) this is an order to be worked throughout the day to get the average price of that day.

Setting and changing a stop-loss

Step 3. Confirming order and specifying the stop-loss level

(See chapters 5 and 8)

Want to change your stop-loss?

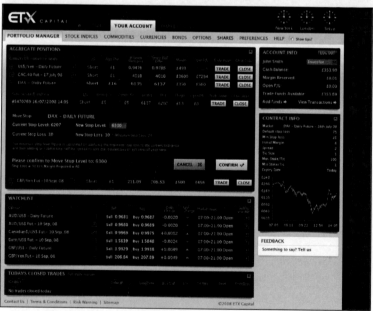

Tracking your trades

Step 4. Tracking your trades and orders

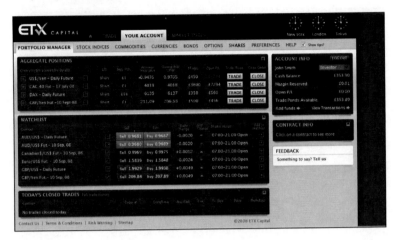

Once the trade has been confirmed, you can view your open positions and the amount of trade funds you have available. You can also monitor your favourite markets all from one page.

Rolling over a trade

Question: What if you want to roll a trade to the next expiry date?

In order for a spread bet to be classified as a bet, it must satisfy some rules. A fixed period is one of them. A **daily bet** expires at the end of the day.

Quarterly bets expire at:

- The end of March
- The end of June
- The end of September
- The end of December

If you have an open position and the contract is nearing expiry, you can:

1. Let the position expire – it will be closed at the official closing price on the expiry day

2. Close the position before expiry

3. Roll over the position

Note: Most spread betting companies offer a special rate to roll a position from one contract to the next. This special offer is usually done during the last few days of the contract period and allows clients to continue running the position without having to pay the dealing costs of trading in and out of the contracts manually.

Example

The Dax March Future contract is trading at 6942 / 6948

The Dax June Future is trading at 7016 / 7022

A long roll would be to close the March contract at mid market 6945 and re-open the June contract at 7022.

This roll would be cheaper then manually closing March at 6942 and manually opening at 7022.

Saving on the roll = 3 points

What you need to know

- In a sense, the term 'rolling over a trade' is misleading because you do have to close the original trade and pay any outstanding balance or pocket your profit. However, rolling over a trade means you save on the dealing costs in the form of a lower spread.

- Roll over instructions should be made at least 30 minutes before the close of the exchange on the day the bet is due to expire. For example, the London Stock Exchange normally closes at 4.30pm.

Key points

- There are different types of orders in spread betting. An order is executed as a trade as and when it meets a set of criteria.

- Use stop-loss orders to limit potential losses.

- You can roll over a trade to the next expiry date.

4

The bid–offer spread explained

"Mind the gap."

– London Underground announcement

The spread bet price vs the underlying price

What is the bid-offer spread?

The bid-offer spread is at the heart of what makes spread betting hassle-free. With traditional share dealing, you have to pay trading-associated fees such as stamp duty (an up front tax charge equivalent to 0.5% of the cost of your share purchase), capital gains tax (a tax on profits), broker commission fees, administration fees and other charges.

By contrast, with spread betting all fees and other trading costs are wrapped within the spread. **All you have to deal with is the price movement**. This chapter will discuss how the spread is determined.

What is the relationship between the spread bet price and the underlying price of the asset?

The spread is derived from the underlying market price (hence the term 'derivatives' when referring to spread betting). For example, the Vodafone June contract is derived from the price that Vodafone shares trade at in the market (called its cash price).

Example

- Vodafone is trading in the stock market at 160.4 / 160.5p. The spread is 0.1p.

- Vodafone June Future is trading at 161.75/162.25p. The spread is 0.5p.

What you need to know

- The spread betting quote in the Vodafone example is wider by an extra 0.4p. This is the spread that the company charges (profit).

- The mid-price for Vodafone shares is 160.455p. The mid-price of the Vodafone December contract is 162p. The 1.545p difference (in this case, a premium) of the Vodafone June contract over Vodafone shares is called the 'cost of carry'. This is the financing cost associated with the trade from the current date to the June expiry date.

The bid-offer spread is calculated differently by the various spread betting companies. For example, some calculate it as a percentage of the cash market price.

To sum up, the future price of a contract is calculated to reflect the cost of carry or interest and dividend payments before the expiry date.

How fast or slow does the spread change?

It changes as fast or as slow as the underlying market. If, for example, Barclays shares rose 30 points during a one hour period, so too would the Barclays June Future.

Because the Barclays June Future is derived from the Barclays share price, it would move up and down in the same direction.

Do not be surprised if a bid-offer spread changes while you are on the phone with your bookmaker. If news comes in about a profit warning or a takeover, and it affects the company you are interested in, either directly or indirectly, the share price may well move, particularly in the minutes after the announcement.

If the product you are trading is an index rather than an individual share, you may see sharp movements if, for example, there is a release of economic data which affects the market's view of the economy. Economic figures often send trading desks into a frenzy.

Daily bets versus future-based bets

The spread may also differ for the same product depending on whether the bet is for a daily contract or a quarterly contract.

Illustration 4.1 – The difference between the spread for a daily versus a quarterly contract

Market	Margin	Spread Requirement	Price
Wall Street Daily Cash	15	5	12686 – 12691
Wall Street Future – Dec 11, 2008	250	7	12707 – 12714

Shopping around for the best deal

Different strokes for different folks. The same principle applies in spread betting. A very important factor when choosing where to trade is the bid-offer spread. Shop around and you will find that different companies may offer different spreads for the same product.

A difference of two tics may seem paltry but if you are staking £1,000 per point, a two-tic difference doesn't seem too small now does it?

Let's compare the quote of three spread betting companies for shares in Barclays:

Name of Company	Company X	Company Y	Company Z
Barclays	493.75p – 495.25p	494p – 498p	492p – 497p

In the above example, company X offers the tightest spread and therefore, the cheapest dealing costs. But if you think shares in Barclays will drop, you might choose company Y because it offers the highest bid (i.e. 494p). However, when it is time to close the position, Y has a wider spread.

Online dealing has made the spread betting market more transparent by allowing traders to easily compare costs. Previously, it was hard to determine who had the best price without making a call to every single company. Now, you just look at their websites.

Other factors to consider when choosing a spread betting company are:

- Online trading, the reliability of their trading platform

- Telephone trading, the quality of their customer service

- The speed of executing the trade either online or by phone

- The range of products you can place a bet on

- Margin requirements

- The type of account you can open (deposit or credit)

- The educational facilities available on their website

- The fundamental analysis research available (some provide institutional research for free to private clients)

- The technical analysis research (charting material) available

- The types of stop-losses and the cost of a guaranteed stop-loss (explained in the next chapter)

- Whether they offer interest on the cash sitting on your account. Just as banks apply a daily interest on your account balance, some spread betting company also credit their clients with interest on their account balance

- Other added-value services such as after-hours support and administration

Spread betting companies may score highly on some criteria but not on others. Often, traders open several accounts and use the company that best suits a particular trade.

Key points

- The spread is derived from the underlying market price (also called its cash price).

- Spread betting companies have different spread quotes.

- Often, traders open several accounts and use the company that best suits a particular trade.

Margin trading explained

"The ultimate risk is not taking a risk."

– Sir James Goldsmith, business tycoon

What is margin trading?

To fully understand the risks and rewards associated with spread betting, you need to be aware that it is a form of margin trading.

Definition:

Margin trading is a form of trading where you only pay a fraction of the actual cost of the trade up front. This is usually 10% in spread betting.

In other words, you only pay **10%** to get exposure to **100%** of the rewards. The result is a higher return on your capital because there is the remaining **90%** that you can choose to leave in the bank or use as capital for something else.

But, by the same token, you only pay **10%** but the **risk involved is the same** as if you have paid **100%** in the first place. If the bet works against your favour, you have to provide extra funds.

By contrast, in conventional share dealing, because you have to put in **100%** at the outset, you have paid the maximum amount that can be lost on the trade.

Here's how it works:

If John buys £10 per point of the FTSE 100 June Future, he would need to deposit around £750 as a down payment or margin. How did we come up with £750? By multiplying £10 by a bet size factor of 75.

This allows the trader to place the trade but is in no way the maximum amount that can be lost on the trade.

To calculate the real exposure of the trade, you multiply the stake (£10 per point) by 6019 (the FTSE 100 index level).

$$6019 \times £10 = \textbf{£60,190} \quad \text{(your worst-case scenario loss)}$$

If the FTSE 100 December Future falls to zero, the total loss on the trade would be £60,019, which is **80 times** more than the £750 John originally deposited.

Note: In reality, the chances of the FTSE 100 falling to zero are as good as nil. Even the calamitous events of September 11th 2001 only wiped the value of the FTSE 100 by 5%. During early 2008, the FTSE 100 fell a total of 371 points, or 18%, during the period between the 4th and 22nd January. It later transpired that SocGen were unwinding their rogue dealer positions at that time. Shares in a company, however, can become almost or even completely worthless, as shareholders in Northern Rock found to their cost as the Bank had to be nationalised following problems in the credit market caused by the US subprime mortgage financial crisis.

What you need to know

- Margin trading is sometimes called **leveraged trading** or **gearing up**. This is because it requires much less capital for the same market exposure.

- In the following example, John only needed £451 to make £100, or a 23% return on his investment. Had he bought the actual shares in Lloyds, £451 would have made £10, or a 2.3% return, on his investment (less the charges).

- However, the risk is substantially higher. Had he bought the actual shares in Lloyds and the share price fell to zero, his total loss would have been £451. At £10 stake per point, his total loss would have been £4,510 (£10 x 451).

> **Example**
>
> John buys £10 pounds per point of Lloyds Bank June Future at 451p.
>
> Total trade value = £4,510, margin required = £451.
>
> Three days later, John sells Lloyds Bank December Future at 461p.
>
> Total profit = £100 (£10 per point 10 points).
>
> Although Lloyds only rose 10 points or 2.2%, John made 22% on his initial investment.
>
> Conversely, he would have lost 22% on a 2.2% movement had he sold rather than bought.

The pros and cons of margin trading

Margin trading at its most perilous is best exemplified by the tales of a derivatives trader at SocGen in early 2008. Trading on the movement of the European indices, his losses mounted to over 4 billion euros. Perhaps he was too young to remember the derivatives trader Nick Leeson, whose similar trading style in the Nikkei lost his employer £1.3 billion, enough to bankrupt Barings Bank.

While these made for movie catastrophies should serve as a dire warning to those who engage in margin trading, it would be unfair to overlook the success stories. Margin trading is not new. Fund managers and banks use it to bulk up or protect their share portfolios. Spread betting, as a form of margin trading, suits those who want to risk a small amount of capital compared to the hundreds of thousands of pounds that fund managers spend.

For example, with spread bets starting from £1 a point, worst-case scenario losses can be as little as £100. At the same time, those who are more experienced can raise the ante to many thousand of pounds per point.

A simple way of describing the risk is this: If you had a pound in your hand and you bet it on a horse and that horse finishes last, **you would have lost £1**.

With margin trading, if you bet a £1 bet on the FTSE, **you could lose £6,000** (i.e. the FTSE index falling from 6,000 points to 0).

The key is for the spread better to calculate the potential losses before they place the bet. Are you comfortable with that level of risk? Can you afford to lose that much?

Risk management

The first rule of spread betting is to preserve your capital

You do this by minimising your losses when the trade goes the wrong way. What may seem like an affordable trade can potentially wipe out your account. For example, if you sell £10 per point of the Dow Jones Index, a rise of 100 points can set you back by £1,000. In 2000, the Dow Jones rose by 200 points soon after AOL announced its merger with Time Warner. This would have resulted in a loss of £2,000 from a seemingly harmless down bet at £10 per point. Such a level of volatility is not uncommon.

To make money, you need to strike a balance between maximising your returns and reducing your risks. The spread betting industry has addressed this issue through a facility called a **stop-loss**.

Definition:

Stop-loss – the level at which a trade is automatically closed to prevent further losses.

Example

On February 25th, John buys £10 per point of the Ladbrokes March contract at 309p, ahead of Ladbrokes' results announcement due a few days away (February 28th).

He thinks the results are going to be good but just in case he is wrong, he sets a stop-loss at 284p.

This stop-loss will close out his position at 284p if the Ladbrokes March contract drops to that level.

This also means that he has limited his downside to 25 points or £250 (25 points multiplied by £10) if he is wrong.

The **margin** for the trade is **£309**.

The value of the trade is £3,090 (Ladbrokes shares falling from 309p to 0 = 309 points x £10).

Before the stop-loss was applied, his downside risk was £1,250. With the stop-loss in place, this was reduced to £250.

John can now benefit from unlimited profits if shares in Ladbrokes rise and, at the same time, cap his potential loss to £250.

Exercise: Let's do the maths

John believes the European Central Bank (ECB) is going to cut rates later in the week, which he thinks will cause the stock markets in Europe to rise. He doesn't know which particular share will rise, so he places his bet on the CAC index of leading French companies.

Mark: Spreadco, Mark speaking, how may I help?

John: Hi Mark. Can I have a quote for the June CAC.

Mark: Hi John, the June CAC is 4937 at 4942.

John: I'd like to buy £20 a point at 4942 please.

Mark: You pay 4942 for £20 per point of June CAC.

John: Oh, I'd like to put a stop-loss on that **50 points** below.

Mark: (repeats the trade back to John)

1. By placing a stop-loss at 4892, what is John's maximum loss?

2. Without the stop-loss, what is John's maximum loss?

3. If the CAC index rises above 4942, what is John's maximum profit?

4. It turns out that the ECB decided to leave the rates unchanged. The market doesn't like the decision and the CAC index slides down to 4747 over the last four hours of the day.

(i) How much cash would John have lost without a stop-loss in place?

(ii) With a stop-loss at 4892, how much did he lose?

Answers to Let's do the maths exercise

1. **£1,000.** This is 50 points x £20 = £1,000.
   (4942 – 4892 = 50 points)

2. His maximum loss would have been the worst-case scenario of the index falling from 4942 to 0 = 4,942 points x £20 bet per point movement = **£98,840**.

3. John's maximum profits is **limitless**. If the CAC index keeps rising, he chooses when to settle the trade and at what profit level.

4. (i) **£3,900**. 4942 – 4747 points = 195 points. The index fell by 195 points, which is not what John expected. Hence, without a stop-loss, he would lose 195 points x £20 = £3,900.

   (ii) Because he had a 50 point stop-loss in place, he only lost **£1,000**, leaving him with an extra £1,900 to continue trading with.

The importance of a stop-loss

What you need to know

A stop-loss is effectively a trade. That means if you place a stop-loss on a buy trade and it turns out it wasn't necessary, you need to tell your spread betting company two things:

1. Close your buy trade with a contra or sell trade.

2. Cancel the stop-loss.

What happens if you forget to cancel a stop-loss order?

In the previous example, if John closed the buy trade and **forgot** to cancel the stop-loss, Spreadco will still have a sell trade outstanding on the CAC 40 index at the stop-loss level of 4892.

If we assume that all of John's trades are automatically settled at the end of the day and the index closed at 4947, he would have lost the equivalent of 55 points or £1,100 to settle the forgotten stop-loss order.

Often, this is settled by talking to the company and explaining the error. However, the heartache and the hassle is not worth it.

> **ALWAYS REMEMBER TO CANCEL THE ASSOCIATED STOP-LOSS ORDERS WITH YOUR TRADES.**

On the other hand, just because you have a stop-loss in place does not mean that you have to close the trade at **that** level.

In the previous example, the CAC 40 index might have risen to 4975 and John might have decided, at that point, to close out for a profit. He is perfectly at liberty to do this. Equally, if he had seen the index falling from 4942 towards 4892, he might have decided to close out for a loss **before** it hit his stop-loss level of 4892. Again, he is perfectly at liberty to do this.

But – and this is important – some spread betting companies require you to cancel a stop-loss when you close out a trade. And if you forget to cancel the stop-loss, it will remain on your account. At ETX Capital, the stop-loss order is **automatically cancelled** when a trade is closed. **Double check with your chosen spread betting company**.

Dialogue 6: Cancelling your stop-loss

Mark: Spreadco, Mark speaking, how may I help?

John: Hi Mark, it's John here, Please quote me the daily FTSE.

Mark: Oh hello John, daily FTSE is 6008 – 6010.

John: Could I please sell £10 to close.

Mark: Sure, you sell £10 daily FTSE at 6008 to close your position.

John: Thanks, I also have a stop-loss in at 5500. Could you please cancel that order for me?

Mark: That's cancelled sir, have a good day.

Guaranteed versus non-guaranteed stop-loss

In an ideal world, the market moves in a straight line. But in reality it doesn't. The price of the share or index you are trading might not trade at your stop-loss level (called to **gap up** or **gap down**). A classic example is when Northern Rock announced it had approached the Bank of England for liquidity support. The shares opened up down £1.25 at £5.20 and then continued to fall closing the day at £4.38, and as if that was not bad enough, when it opened the following Monday another £1.18 had been wiped off the stock.

A **non-guaranteed stop-loss is free** but, as the term suggests, the spread betting company does not guarantee that it can close the trade at the exact level you indicated.

By contrast, a **guaranteed stop-loss** will, for an extra charge in the form of a wider spread, close a trade at the pre-determined level even if the price gaps over this figure.

A guaranteed stop is only available at the time of opening the bet. Some spread betting companies allow you to change the level of the guaranteed stop as long as it is not lower than the minimum stop level. For example, for a daily FTSE, the minimum stop is 40 points. So a guaranteed stop has to be more than 40 points if you want to re-adjust it after opening the bet.

Some spread betting companies also allow you to change the level of the guaranteed stop as long as it is at least 5% away from the opening bet level.

What you need to know

Many traders find that a non-guaranteed stop-loss is more than adequate to limit their losses.

However, a **guaranteed stop-loss is very useful in extremely volatile** markets.

The term 'extremely volatile' is hard to define. What is a volatile market for one person may not be volatile for another. The concept will be described in more detail later but, in simple terms, you would expect a stock or an index to be volatile based on their historic chart performance (i.e. a history of large price movements).

The extra charge for a guaranteed stop varies but may be two tics or more added to a regular bid-offer quote.

Table 5.1 – Difference between the spread for a guaranteed and a non-guaranteed stop-loss

For the daily FTSE index (FTSE 100) and Daily FTSE Future

IG Index Spread		Controlled Risk Spread on Guaranteed Stop	
Trading hours*	Outside trading hours	Trading hours*	Outside trading hours
6	8	8	10

* Trading hours means from 8am to 4.30pm.

What you need to know

- If you were to trade the FTSE during trading hours, the spread for a trade with a non-guaranteed stop attached is 6 points. Outside trading hours, the spread goes up to 8 points.

- If you were to trade with a **guaranteed stop**, the trade costs two tics more. The table shows that the spread is **8 points** and **10 points** respectively for during trading hours and outside trading hours.

- A **controlled risk spread**, where a trade comes with a guaranteed stop-loss, needs a **reduced deposit**. For example, if you want to put a £10 per point buy on the June FTSE opened at 6000. The normal deposit required is £3,000 (£10 x 300 bet size factor). If a stop is placed at 5950, the deposit factor used would drop to 110.*

Other types of stop-loss

Mandatory stop-loss

At spread betting company ETX Capital, clients have to place a stop-loss with all their trades. The company believes a stop-loss is a necessary tool of risk management.

If you are trading online, all trades automatically come with a default stop-loss. You can customise it to your desired level.

The stop-loss is **not guaranteed**. However, ETX Capital says that in the vast majority of cases, they execute the stop-loss, as indicated.

A mandatory stop-loss has its advantages and disadvantages. One advantage is that you limit your potential losses on a trade. A disadvantage is that you may be stopped out from momentary, but large, price movements.

---

* Example from IG Index. The deposit factor is calculated as 50 (the distance of the stop) plus 60 (20% of 300, the normal deposit factor). So, 110 x £10 = £1,100.

The trick is to set your stop-loss such that it allows for 'wriggle movement'.* That is, it is far enough from your starting level so that you don't get stopped out sooner than you planned.

Trailing stop-loss

Suppose you place a buy bet on an index and the price of that index starts rising, nothing to worry about so far. But then the price moves to a point where you think it might start falling. One way to lock-in your profits before the imminent fall is to put a **trailing stop-loss** on your trade.

Example

John buys £10 per point of Starbucks at 1920. He leaves a stop at 1820 (100 tics away).

- Maximum possible loss is £1,000 (£10 x 100 = £1,000).

- If Starbucks moves down, the trade will be stopped out with a maximum loss of £1,000.

- If Starbucks moves up to 2120 (a rise of 200 tics), John raises his stop from 1820 to 2020. This locks in a 100 tic profit and allows him to benefit from any further increase of Starbucks' share price.

- If Starbucks continues to move up, John may want to continue to raise the stop level – continually increasing the locked-in profit.

Spread betting companies do not offer automatic trailing stops. You have to set it yourself by raising your stop-loss level as and when the market moves up.

---

* See case study on Patrick Gray on page 122. Allowing for wriggle movement is part of his spread betting strategy.

Key points

- The risk and reward profile of margin trading, such as spread betting, is different to conventional share trading.

- To limit your potential losses, use a stop-loss as a risk management tool.

- There are two types of stop-loss: guaranteed and non-guaranteed.

- Your stop-loss is triggered when the market reaches that level.

- Move your stop-losses to lock in profits.

Tools of the trade

"Give us the tools and we will finish the job."

– **Winston Churchill, 1941**

Spread betting is not a black art. There are financial tools at your disposal to increase your chances of making the right call. How? By doing your research and understanding buy and sell signals.

There are two types of analysis to predict price movements. These are:

1. **Fundamental**

2. **Technical**

1. **Fundamental** – valuing a company's share based on information about its financial and operational performance.

    As the term suggests, you have to analyse the 'fundamentals' such as:

    - The company's cash flow profile
    - How the company operates
    - The debts and assets on its balance sheet
    - The management's investment strategy

    One of the most popular yardsticks that investors use is the price-to-earnings (P/E) ratio.

    > Price-to-Earnings = share price / earnings per share

    Fundamental analysis is explained in greater detail later in this chapter.

2. **Technical** – using statistical data such as past prices and trading volumes to judge where the share price is going to be in the future.

    With technical analysis, it is irrelevant whether the company makes widgets or provides cleaning services. Rather, you look at charts and study the pattern to predict future trends.

    It is argued that all of the information necessary to predict tomorrow's prices can be drawn from the sequence of yesterday's prices.

    There are numerous software programs that allow you to monitor a stock's technical data (see Appendix 4). The most basic charts are described later in this chapter.

This section aims to name and briefly explain the fundamental and technical data commonly used in spread betting. It serves as a taster, not a comprehensive catalogue. Website addresses for further reading are in Appendix 4.

Fundamental Analysis

Examples

---

1. Price-to-Earnings ratio (P/E) and Earnings per share (EPS)

The price-to-earnings ratio (P/E) is calculated by dividing the share price by the company's full year earnings per share (EPS), and is a measure of how expensive the company's shares are for every £1 profit it makes.

As a rule of thumb, the higher the P/E ratio, the more expensive the company's shares are, and the lower the P/E the cheaper they are. Companies with very high or very low P/Es should be treated with caution.

A company's P/E is only meaningful when you compare it against the average P/E in the sector it belongs to, or against the P/E ratio of a competitor.

For example, services company ABC has a P/E of 12 times, while construction company XYZ plc has a P/E of 9 times. Which one do you think is cheaper?

You would think construction company XYZ plc is cheaper.

However, it could be that in the construction sector, the average P/E of all the companies is 5, which means that XYZ plc is nearly twice as expensive as the average listed construction company.

The lesson to takeaway here is to make sure you compare apples with apples.

If you use the latest full year EPS in your calculations then you are looking at the **historic P/E**. If you use the forecast earnings per share (estimated earnings per share of the company according to analysts) then you are looking at its **prospective** or **forward P/E**.

Example

The share price of company ABC: 100p

Earnings per share in the previous financial year: 10p

Estimated earnings per share in the next financial year: 20p

Historic price-to-earnings ratio (P/E) = 100p / 10p = **10**

Forecast or prospective P/E = 100p / 20p = **5**

On its own, this ratio is meaningless. You have to compare it to the P/E ratio of companies in the same sector.

- Is ABC's P/E higher or lower than that of its competitors?

- Is ABC's P/E higher or lower than the sector average?

Example

In February 2008, Tesco Plc had a P/E of 15.72, while Sainsbury Plc had a P/E of 17.08.

Based on fundamental data, you could say that Tesco is **undervalued** relative to Sainsbury.

Or, Sainsbury is **overvalued** relative to Tesco.

2. Sales figures

In sales-driven sectors such as retailers and electrical, many traders make decisions based on **expected sales figures**. For example, the share price of high street retailers such as Marks & Spencer will react to good or bad Christmas sales figures. The share price of mobile phone maker Vodafone Group also depends on its mobile handset sales.

If you do not have access to the financial websites of Bloomberg or Datastream, two sites that provide forecast and historic sales figures are Yahoo! Finance (⌨ http://uk.finance.yahoo.com) and Hemscott (⌨ www.hemscott.com).

3. Net Asset Value (NAV) per share

Suppose you are a billionaire scouting for a nuts-and-bolts manufacturing company, what is the minimum amount you would be willing to pay for a company?

In crude terms, you would probably pay the equivalent of the value of that company's factory, plus the nuts and bolts in stock minus the company's outstanding debts.

What you have just calculated is called a company's net asset value or NAV.

Analysts and fund managers alike often use the NAV per share as the minimum amount they would pay for a certain stock. Traders often hunt for companies that are trading below their NAV per share. The argument being; if at worst the company goes belly up and has to be sold, traders will still get a higher amount than they paid for.

Put another way, when a company is trading at a price that is lower than its net asset value per share (for example, if company XYZ Plc has a share price of 88p but its net asset value is 100p) then punters might put a buy bet in the hope that the shares will catch up with the company's NAV per share.

Even if they don't, and the company gets liquidated, these punters have a high chance of exiting at a profit.

Often, the share price catches up with the company's NAV per share.

Example

In March 2003, shares in Kingfisher were trading at 130p. This gave the company a market capitilisation of approximately £3bn. At the time, the company's assets less current liabilities valued it at £4.4bn. That is, the company had a Net Asset Value of 188p per share.

Fundamentally, the company was cheap and the market was eventually coming round to acknowledging this, as it received upgrades from brokers and embarked on a share buy back programme. As a result, the stock began its advance upwards.

4. Dividends / Dividend yield

Dividend yield, the traditional yardstick in the share market, has its fans in spread betting. It is calculated by taking a company's dividend per share (historic or forecast) and dividing this figure by the company's share price.

Example

In February 2008, UK communications company BT had a 12 month yield of 6.72%, the dividend for 2007 was 15.4p versus a share price of 229p (15.4 / 229 = 0.0672).

By contrast, one of its main competitors, Cable & Wireless was yielding 3.74%. On that basis BT looked very attractive compared to C&W.

Other buy/sell signals

---

1. Directors' dealings

Action speaks louder than words. When directors, chief executives and chairmen buy shares in their companies, traders often treat this as a positive signal and follow suit. When directors sell, alarm bells ring, and the bears are not far behind.

All directors' dealings are reported to the London Stock Exchange and can be found on their regulatory news service (💻 www.rns.com).

However, you can save some time by going directly to financial websites Hemscott (💻 www.hemscott.com), and Money AM (💻 www.moneyam.com), trade magazines and spread betting companies (they often have their own set of research). The normal layout is:

*   Name of company

*   Name of director

- Number of shares bought or sold

- Price they were bought or sold

- Total number of shares held by the director after the transaction

- Percentage of the director's holding relative to the total shareholding of the company (e.g. whether he is a 5% stakeholder)

In some cases, the dealings have nothing to do with the company's performance or prospects but are brought about by the director's personal affairs. For example, the director may have sold some shares to fund a purchase or pay for a wedding. To check whether a director's trade is relevant or not, you should:

- *Compare the number of shares bought or sold relative to that of the director's total shareholding.*

  If a director buys or sells only a very small percentage in relation to his total holding, the trade is unlikely to affect the share price.

- Check the dealing price. This may give you an inkling of the director's view of the company's valuation.

  For example, if a director buys shares at 100p, you should gather historical data on the share price. Compare the price he bought at (100p) to the 52-week low, 52-week high, all-time low and all-time high. All these prices are freely available (see Appendix 4).

  If a director bought the shares at 100p and the 52-week high was 200p, then that would be a different story than if he bought them at 100p and the 52-week high was 95p.

2. Brokers consensus estimates

Depending on the size of a company, there can be one to half a dozen brokers that analyse it. These analysts will periodically publish their research and provide a recommendation on the stock which might be a buy, a sell or a hold.

Other terms are sometimes used, but they all boil down to buy, sell or hold.

The analysts' recommendations will be based on:

- The company's profit/cash flow numbers (current and forecast)

- Their opinion on the prospects of the company (e.g. whether its new product range will be successful or whether it is capable of meeting profit targets)

- Their view on whether the share price reflects the value of the company

- Their view on whether the share price undervalues or overvalues the company relative to its competitors

It used to be the case that analyst research was only available to big clients of the brokers that employ the analysts. It was the brokers' way of trying to attract institutional business. In recent years, however, financial websites and magazines have started making broker research available, sometimes for free and sometimes for a fee. Some spread betting companies offer their clients access to research that is normally only available to institutions.

Even if you cannot get the detailed research, you can usually find the consensus forecasts. This is an amalgam of all the individual forecasts to produce a single view.

The theory is that if nine analysts think that Company X is a buy, then that is more reliable than the view of just one analyst who thinks it's a sell. Of course there will always be exceptions.

Consensus forecasts are widely reported on the internet and in investor magazines.

Technical analysis

Some traders like to think of the market as a series of numbers or statistical data, also called **technical analysis**. The theory being you can predict the price movement of a share or an index based on how it has performed historically.

The most popular technical weapon of choice is **charting**, where the price of a stock or an index is plotted as points over a given time period. By doing so, a trader gets an idea of whether the price has consistently gone up, down or stayed flat over time.

The argument is that prices exhibit patterns over a period of time. If you can read the signs, then you can time when to buy or when to sell.

Technical analysts also believe that price changes can only be sustained by **heavy trading volume** (the number of shares traded over a given time). That is why traders look at both price movement and trading volume to ascertain whether a security is a buy or a sell.

Note that there are some traders who look at charts based on price movement over five-minute intervals, and those that look at it on a daily, three-month or even longer interval.

Beginners should start with basic charting patterns established over a longer period of time (e.g. 3-months, 1-year, 3-years).

In this section, we look at basic charts. Many books are devoted to technical analysis and you should take a look at them if you wish to explore this topic further.

In brief, charts will guide you as to whether a price is in an uptrend or a downtrend.

Here, we look at:

1. Resistance levels

2. Support

3. Trend lines

4. Golden cross

Examples

1. Resistance level – used as a sell signal. This is the level a share price reaches before it starts falling.

The theory is that if a share price has repeatedly failed in the past to climb above a certain level, there is resistance among traders and investors to buying above that level.

You can also look at the resistance level as a sign that there is an increased supply of shares in the market, pushing the price down.

Example

The chart of the FTSE 100 index below shows a good example of strong resistance at the 6750 level. Note how the price repeatedly tested this level, running out of steam and falling sharply.

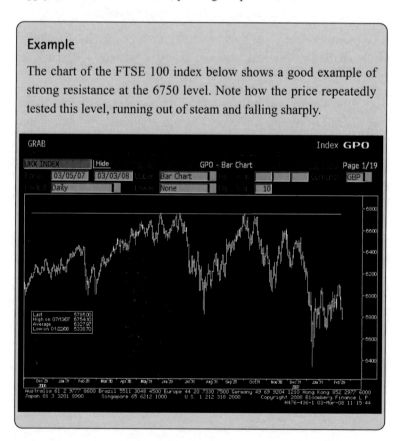

2. Support – used as a buy signal. This is the range of prices that a stock or an index will fall to before it reverses to an uptrend (a price rise).

When it breaks through this level, a new trading range is established.

The reasoning behind this is that a price reaches the support level because the second round of buyers have decided to buy in the shares after the first round of buyers have decided to take profits.

Example

The chart below shows a graph of £/$ or 'cable' as it is commonly known in the City. It is a good example of repeated support at the 1.9350 level, creating a 'triple bottom'. Look to buy on any strong rallies from support levels.

3. Trend lines – used as a buy or sell signal. A market will establish a downward or upward pattern over a period of time.

Example

The chart below is a long-term (monthly) graph of Diageo. As we can see, once the upward trend was established, marked out by the trendline, Diageo offered potentially low-risk buy signals. This uptrend lasted more than two years, providing traders with plenty of profitable opportunities. It wasn't until January 2008 when the stock broke to the downside quite strongly and ended its positive bias. But as a result, it gave traders the chance to go short and jump on a potential downward trend.

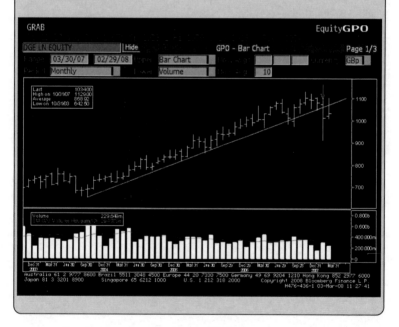

4. Golden cross – used as a buy signal. Occurs when the shorter term moving average* (black line) crosses through the longer term moving average† (grey line) while the longer term is showing gentle incline. **BUY at the cross.**

* 50-day moving average. This plots the average price of a stock over the past 50 days. Technical analysts argue that a change in the direction of the 50-day moving average means a change in the demand for that stock.

† 200-day moving average. This plots the average price of a stock over the past 200 days.

Key points

- Use fundamental data and charts to predict price movements.

- Two fundamental data that traders use are the P/E ratio and the dividend yield.

- Basic charting patterns to look out for are called **resistance, support, trend lines and the golden cross**.

7

The big picture

"No man is an island, entire of itself."

— **John Donne, 17th century English poet**

Three concepts often mentioned when discussing the market are:

- Economy
- Liquidity
- Volatility

This chapter will explain these central themes and how they can affect your spread bets.

Economy

Now that you know the basics, it is time to learn how the financial wealth or economy of a region influence stock and bond market movements.

This topic hardly makes for exciting dinner conversation but is very important. Think of economic indicators, such as interest rates or unemployment rates, as traffic lights – signalling when to press the accelerator or put the brakes on.

The Financial Times website (🖳 www.ft.com) is invaluable as it provides a brief description of what the economic indicators are, when they are due and how they influence the rise and fall of the market.

To start with, keep track of the following:

1. Interest rate changes

The US Federal Open Market Committee (FOMC), currently chaired by Ben Bernanke, sets the interest rate, called the **Fed Funds** rate. This serves as a bellwether for all other interest rates such as mortgage loan repayments and interest paid on government bonds. The impact of the Fed Funds rate is far-reaching. It can influence interest rates in other financial markets such as the UK, called the Monetary Policy Committee (MPC) rate, and the rest of Europe called the European Central Bank (ECB) rate. However, the subprime crisis led the FOMC to dramatically cut rates in late 2007 and early 2008, which was not mirrored across the pond.

What you need to know

The FOMC meets around every six weeks and the market speculates in advance whether they will change the Fed Funds rate or not.

As a rule of thumb, a rise in interest rates is not good for the stock market because increased interest cost reduces corporate profits. A fall in interest rates is good for the stock market because it is cheaper for companies to borrow money, and lower interest cost means higher profits.

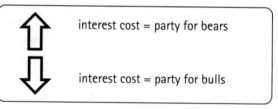

⬆ interest cost = party for bears

⬇ interest cost = party for bulls

However, it does not follow that a rise in interest rate always leads to a fall in stock markets. The key is expectations. If market watchers have anticipated the rise, then the impact of such a rate increase has been factored into share prices ahead of the rate change.

Example

How the market reacts to the FOMC meeting.

John thinks that the FOMC will surprise the market with a small interest rate cut in its January announcement. Because the market is not anticipating the cut, he thinks it will be very bullish and that the market as a whole will gain ground.

He buys £10 per point of the DOW daily at 12650.

At 7:15pm UK time the FOMC announces that rates will fall by 0.25 basis points.

As he expected the market moves quickly upwards 150 points and he closes out at 12800 with a profit of £1,500 (£10 x 150).

---

2. Retail sales

Consumer spending is the oil that greases the wheels of the economy. If you keep track of what consumers are spending on, how much they spend and whether their spending has gone up or down, you'll have a fair idea of where the economy is headed.

Also, retail sales figures will help you scan the market for the sectors that are doing well (buy) or doing badly (sell). For example, clothing sales figures are up, so you would look at placing up bets on high street retailers such as Next or Marks and Spencer.

3. Jobless claims

In the US, the jobless claims figure is a weekly compilation of the number of individuals who have filed for **unemployment benefits**. The less number of people filing for unemployment means more people have jobs and therefore, more people have income. Using a simple diagram, we can illustrate this as:

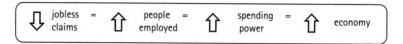

However, the saying "too much of a good thing can be bad" holds true. Spread betters should adjust their trades if the number of job seekers fall to such a level that companies find it hard to hire new workers or pay more to retain their existing staff.

⬆ jobless = ⬆ labour = wage = interest = ⬇ company
   claims   costs   inflation rate rise   profits

4. US non-farm payrolls

You watch non-farm payrolls for the same reason you watch jobless claims figures. That is, you want a good handle on the rate of employment and unemployment and therefore, consumer spending. In brief, non-farm payroll figures indicate the basic hourly wages for major industries. It shows who are unemployed, who are working, how much they are getting paid and how many hours they work per week.

Despite its boring name, non-farm payroll figures keep the financial markets on both sides of the Atlantic on their toes. In a diagram:

Non-farm payrolls = wage trends = possibility of wage inflation

Wage inflation = ⬆ interest rate = party for bears

No wage inflation = ⬇ or = interest rate = bears/bulls

What you need to know ─────────────

As a UK spread better, why do you need to monitor both the UK and the US economic indicators?

This is because the UK business activity is closely interlinked with the US. More importantly, the US economy is the largest in the world, with a gross domestic product of over $13 trillion – 20% of the world's total.

Liquidity

The term 'liquidity', as used here, refers to how easy it is to buy or sell a particular security.

In shares, liquidity is determined by:

Market capitalisation

The value of a company measured as the number of its shares multiplied by its share price.

For example, Vodafone has 53.125 billion shares and a share price of 160.5p (as at February 28th 2008)

Vodafone's market capitalisation = 53.125 billion shares x 160.5p

= £85.267 billion

In shares, as a rule of thumb, the bigger the company the higher the number of shares to trade and therefore the more liquid the shares are.

For example, Vodafone, with a market capitalisation of £85.267 billion and 53.125 billion shares is more liquid than JKX Oil & Gas, with a market capitalisation of £727 million and 156 million shares (as at February 28th, 2008).

However, this is not always the case. For example, company ABC may have a larger market capitalisation than company XYZ even if they both have an equal number of shares if company ABC has a higher share price.

> **Why do you need to check a market's liquidity?**
>
> **Broadly speaking, the more liquid the asset, the narrower the spread. And, the less liquid the asset, the wider the spread.**

Using a pond as an analogy, a highly liquid stock is like a big, deep pond. It has space for a larger number of investors who can dip in and out without individually making a big impact on the pond.

By contrast, an illiquid share is like a small, shallow pond. It can only accommodate a limited number of investors and therefore, is not as easy to buy or sell. An individual can also make a big impact on the pond.

Taking the JKX and Vodafone comparison, imagine an institution trying to buy ten million shares in both companies. To JKX, that makes up 6.4% of its total share holding. To Vodafone, ten million shares makes up around 0.019% of its total share holding.

What are the implications?

To JKX, the institution's purchase should push the share price up (good), however, with an average trading amount of 775k shares per day it will not be likely that it could sell all ten million shares to profit from the price increase, and indeed trying to sell them will likely force the price back down (bad).

By contrast, Vodafone's share price moves due to factors other than the institution's purchase (good). Also, because a ten million holding is a fraction of the 235 million traded on average per day, the institution will have no problem selling its holding (good).

The catch-22 situation here is that small companies (i.e. small market capitalisation, less liquidity) enjoy faster growth rates than large companies (i.e. good for share price).

In the end, you have to make the judgement call. But if you are a beginner, steer clear of non-liquid shares.

Again, the more liquid the asset, the narrower the spread and therefore the cheaper it is to trade.

The less liquid the asset, the wider the spread and therefore the more expensive it is to trade.

Volatility

In spread betting, volatility is a necessary evil. You want prices to go up or down at a magnitude that is enough to cover the cost of the spread and to make profits, but at the same time, you do not want the price to be so volatile as to wipe your capital if the price moves against you.

So, how do you tread the fine line between volatile and not too volatile?

There is no quick and easy answer. On one hand, volatility can be measured* and therefore, you can pick and choose a security depending on its volatility figure.

---

* Volatility is a measure of the probability of price movements, expressed as a percentage. For example, say the gold price is 423.5p and its historical volatility is 20%. A volatility of 20% means there is a high probability (arbitrarily 68%) that gold will trade between 338.8p and 508.2p (20% either side of 423.5p) over a one year period. If the volatility rises to 30%, then gold will have a high probability of trading at a wider range.

On the other hand, this figure is based on historical data and the risk is that a security's volatility veers away from the average!

In the end, preserving your capital is everything, so cap your potential losses by placing a stop-loss on all your trades.

In spread betting the rule of thumb is to look at the volatility of an asset in percentage terms for the day (for daily bets).

Key points

- Changes in the US interest rate (the Fed Funds rate) is the bench mark for all other major interest rates around the world.

- The more liquid the stock, the narrower the spread.

- Use a stop-loss order to limit your potential losses when the market is very volatile.

Spread betting strategies

"Small opportunities are often the beginning of great enterprises."

– Demosthenes, Greek orator

In this chapter, we will look at five types of spread betting strategies namely, shorting, hedging, momentum trading, pairs trading and arbitrage.

Get shorting

Definition: selling securities you do not own in the hope of buying them back at a lower price in the future and pocketing the difference.

Example

John thinks shares in XYZ Plc are going to fall from their current price of 450p.

He enters a contract to **sell** them at 450p in three months time.

The price falls from 450p to 400p after three months.

He **buys** the shares at 400p making an 11% profit
(450 – 400 = 50 / 450).

If his bet was for £10 per point, the profit would have been
50 x £10 = £500.

With shorting, the risk is that the price moves upwards during the time period of the bet.

In the example above if the price rose to 480p, John would have had to close his bet by buying at that price. His loss would then have been 30 points (450 – 480) and, assuming that the bet was for £10 per point, he would be down £300.

In ordinary share trading, there has always been a psychological barrier to shorting. 'Selling something you do not own' was felt to be improper, almost unpatriotic, and somehow not in the spirit of investing.

This hostility is quite irrational, since 'shorting' is an everyday part of many business transactions. When you pre-book a turkey for Christmas, the butcher is effectively selling short – selling something which he does not yet own.

If you buy a house on a greenfield site from a property developer when all the company has at that time is a block of land and a building plan, the property developer is selling you a house that does not exist yet.

You should dismiss the thought that shorting is an unorthodox way of trading, or a kind of exotic activity reserved for hedge funds and sophisticated traders. It isn't. It is simply the reverse side of going long, and a way to back your view that a price is likely to go down.

Think of it this way:

– If you only ever go long on shares (buy before you sell), you can only make money from price advances.
– If you have shorting in your armoury, you can profit from price falls as well.

As we all know, markets can fall as well as rise, so it makes sense to be as comfortable going short on the markets as you are going long.

In spread betting, shorting is equivalent to placing a sell on a market. The way you profit is exactly the same way as when you buy. If the price falls by 10 points then your profit is 10 points multiplied by your stake.

Example

John walks into a branch of a listed hardware company – Hammer Co. – and notices that there are less people lining up to buy items from the store than in previous weeks. John follows the shares of Hammer Co. and remembers that the company is due to release a trading update in a few weeks.

He predicts that Hammer Co. will lower their sales targets based on his research and what he witnessed at the branch. He places a down bet at £50 per point at 130p.

As he rightly predicted, Hammer Co. announced weaker than expected sales over the latest quarter. The share price falls to 110p and John makes a gain of 20 points (130p-110p) x £50 = £1,000.

Hedging

Definition: hedging is protecting an existing holding or asset, should it fall in value, by making an equivalent investment that offsets or reduces potential losses. This allows you to leave your share holding undisturbed in the event of an unexpected price fall.

Spread betting is often used to hedge a physical share portfolio against short-term falls in the market.

It is much cheaper to do this than to sell the entire portfolio and buy it back at a later stage.

Example

John owns a portfolio of mainly FTSE 100 shares with a total value of £60,000.

He thinks the FTSE 100 index is going to fall. He could back his judgement by selling his shares, waiting for the market to fall, then buying them back at the lower price. The problem for John is that he has large gains on his portfolio, and if he sells the shares, a capital gains tax charge will arise.

An alternative is to hedge his portfolio against a fall by selling the FTSE 100 index short. The idea here is that if the FTSE does fall as expected, any drop in the value of the individual shares in John's portfolio will be offset by profits he makes by going short on the index. Let's say that John takes the spread betting route and see what the effect would be:

Action: He sells £10 per point of the FTSE 100 future at 6000 points, when the quote on the index is 6000 – 6005.

Scenario 1: The FTSE 100 drops by 10% to 5400

Assuming that John's individual shares all fell by the same % as the index, his portfolio would drop in value by £6000 to £54,000.

– If John closes his spread bet by buying the FTSE 100 Future at 5,400, his gain would be (6000 – 5400) x £10 = £6,000.

In other words, his portfolio losses would be matched by profits from his short position.

Scenario 2: The FTSE does not drop, but stays at 6000

– If the FTSE does not fall as John expects, but stays at 6000, and assuming that his individual shares reflect the index, his share portfolio would be unchanged in value at £60,000.

– When John comes to close his short position by buying back the FTSE 100 Future he will have to do so at the higher side of the spread, let's say 6005. His loss of the spread bet will be limited to the spread of 5 points x £10 = £60.

Scenario 3: The FTSE does not drop, but rises to 6200

– If John's prediction is completely wrong and the FTSE rises to 6200, his share portfolio will rise in value in proportion to a value of £62,000.

– His losses on the spread bet will be approximately the same. He will have to buy back the FTSE at 6205, and will make a loss of £2,050 (£10 per point on the difference between 6000 and 6205).

There are several key points to note about this hedge:

1. Because it was set up as a counterweight to John's share portfolio, whatever the market did (whether it went up, down or sideways), his overall position was largely unaffected. The hedge kept him in a market-neutral position.

2. It enabled John to take precautions against a market fall without actually selling his shares and incurring capital gains tax.

3. The price of that insurance was low. In the situation where the FTSE did not move, John's cost was just £50. He may have been wrong about the FTSE, but having the hedge in place gave him peace of mind on his share portfolio and, at just £50, he may have felt that that was worth paying.

Momentum trading

When something is described as gathering momentum, the image of a snowball growing larger as it rolls downhill comes to mind.

In the share market, momentum trading works in the same vein. A trader will either buy or sell on a market when there appears to be more activity (on the buy or sell side), other traders follow suit and it becomes a self-feeding mechanism.

The key to momentum trading is finding out **trading volumes; the actual number of those buying and those selling, and in what amounts.** Traders can find out this information if they have access to what is called Level II data. This data is the entire breadth of information available from the stock exchange. These days, private investors can afford to subscribe to Level II services.

Example

Clothing retailer New Look Plc is quoted in the market at 334 – 338. Over the past two hours, most of the volume is changing hands at 338p.

A momentum trader would take this as a buy signal. The view is that because most trades are buy trades, the share is going to go up.

Example

Similarly, when looking at the order book (Level II data) of a share, there may be tell tale signs that a particular share is going up or down.

The graph below shows the Level II order book for Drax, the electricity generator.

You can see that there are more sellers than buyers at this particular time, indicating that supply is exceeding demand and the stock could sell off further.

GRAB					EquityBBO	

At 12:05 Vol 859,827 Op 570 L Hi 576.5 L Lo 549.5 L Prev 581
1 <GO> Calculator   2 <GO> Change View   3 <GO> Yellow Strip   ▐ 4 <GO> Montage View ▌

BEST BID AND OFFER

DRX LN   Drax Group PLC   GBp
🏴🇬🇧   NMS 6.25 Sector 25FS Segment STMM Period SMMP
          Intraday AT Trade Volume 853587

	BID		ASK	
Size	Price	Price		Size
2641	1 **549.5**	**550.5**	6	5201
500	1 549	**549.5** 551	1	545
5439	3 548.5	859827 551.5	3	1404
2189	4 547	552	1	505
9510	1 543.5	552.5	2	4633
9884	1 538	553	3	600
10038	1 530.5	555	3	6459
		556	1	6110
		557	2	12798
		560	1	2000

Australia 61 2 9777 8600 Brazil 5511 3048 4500 Europe 44 20 7330 7500 Germany 49 69 9204 1210 Hong Kong 852 2977 6000
Japan 81 3 3201 8900   Singapore 65 6212 1000   U.S. 1 212 318 2000   Copyright 2008 Bloomberg Finance L.P.
H476-436-1 03-Mar-08 12:06:12

Pairs trading

A pairs trade or a hedge trade is one in which you go long on one share and short on another in the same sector. The theory is that as both of the shares are in the same sector, they will move in the same direction (up or down). However, if one company is perceived as stronger than another, then the stronger company enjoys a higher price rise than the weaker company.

For example, let's take the telecommunications sector and assume that the market is bullish about its prospects. Suppose we pick two companies in the sector, Cable ABC Plc and Cable XYZ Plc. If Cable ABC Plc has posted rising profits over the last three years while Cable XYZ Plc posted a profit warning only two months ago, then we can safely say that Cable ABC Plc is the stronger company.

How do you do a pairs trade?

Example

Action: You buy Cable ABC Plc and sell Cable XYZ Plc.

Scenario 1: The telecommunications sector enjoys a re-rating. Shares in both Cable ABC Plc and XYZ Plc go up. More specifically, shares in Cable ABC Plc rise by 10% while shares in Cable XYZ Plc rise by 3%.

Result: Profit gain from Cable ABC Plc compensates for losses in the down bet for Cable XYZ Plc.

Scenario 2: The telecommunications sector enjoys a re-rating. Shares in both Cable ABC Plc and Cable XYZ Plc go up. More specifically, shares in Cable ABC Plc rise by 10% while shares in Cable XYZ Plc also rise by 10%.

Result: Break even.

Scenario 3: The telecommunications sector does not enjoy a re-rating, but contrary to expectations suffers a de-rating. Shares in both Cable ABC Plc and Cable XYZ Plc go down. More specifically, shares in Cable ABC Plc fall by 10% while shares in Cable XYZ Plc fall by 15%.

Result: Profit gain from the down bet on Cable XYZ Plc compensate for losses in the up bet for Cable ABC Plc.

Example

Opinion: In January 2007, John decided that Kazakhmys was overpriced in its sector.

Action: He placed a sell bet in Kazakhmys and a buy in Xstrata, hoping that Xstrata would outperform Kazakhmys over the year. By placing a pairs trade, he was not directly exposed to overall market risk because he was effectively hedged. If the sector fell, he would make profits on Kazakhmys and lose on Xstrata.

Result: The pairs trade was a success. Whilst Kazakhmys rose from 1000 to 1374 (37%), Xstrata rose from 2200 to 3600 (63.6%) over the year.

Example

Instead of betting on two companies in the same sector, a pairs trade can also be done on two companies from different sectors, for example, one from a cyclical sector and another from an anti-cyclical sector. In particular, one stock is in retailing and the other is a utility.

In pairs trading, the aim is to profit from one share outperforming the other.

Arbitrage

As discussed in chapter 4, different spread betting companies set their own quotes and this can lead to one quoting a more favourable bid-offer price than another for the same product. This provides 'arbitrage opportunities' where traders pocket the difference by buying one quote and selling the other.

Online trading has made it easier to compare quotes from different providers so arbitrage opportunities are few and far between. **It is not a recommended exercise for novices.**

Key points

- You can hedge your traditional portfolio by placing an equivalent short spread bet in the same or similar market

- Momentum trading is about the underlying sentiment of the market whether it is bullish or bearish.

- Arbitrage activity is not for beginners.

Facts or feelings?

"We are what we repeatedly do. Excellence then is not an act, but a habit."

– Aristotle, Greek philosopher

Pretend that you are watching a show, e.g. something on the Discovery Channel featuring two beasts – a lion cub (the amateur spread better) and a fully-grown adult leopard (the professional trader). Faced with the same crisis, our protagonists behave differently. If you think you belong to the lion cub camp, this section will show you the trading mentality that can help you survive the stock market jungle.

Fund managers, brokers, traders and spread betting experts, all concur that the golden rules to live by are:

- The trend is your friend

- Run profits

- Cut losses

Clichés they may be, but very effective ones. Ignore them at your cost. Unfortunately, it is human nature to do the opposite. Novice traders tend to:

- Defy the trend

- Take profits early

- Let losses run

Usually, it is through painful and expensive experience that a trader would make the leap and adopt a different mental strategy.

It is common knowledge that professional day traders tend to run their profits and make incremental losses. The rationale is that they abide by the law of averages. To preserve their capital, their overall profits must offset their overall losses.

Successful trading is **10% technical and 90% psychological**. If you smash through the mental barriers then you are more likely to achieve your financial goals.

Of course you should follow these rules with some flexibility. They are there as your guide, not your straitjacket.

The first golden rule mentioned, 'the trend is your friend', is self-explanatory. Recall that in the charting section in chapter 6, investors watch whether prices are going up or down (trend lines).

In addition, momentum trading (explained in chapter 8) is about traders piling into where the money is – heavy trading volumes.

Of course, bucking the trend has its merits. But in spread betting, the probability of making money lies firmly on predicting what the trend is and betting on that pattern rather than against it.

Let us focus on the other two rules: run your profits and cut your losses.

Run with the rally

A common mistake of inexperienced traders is to take profits too early. As they become more experienced, they realise that overall returns are improved by running profitable trades that little bit further.

However, the market does not stay in one direction forever. So when do you take profits?

When to take profits

a) Due to fundamental data

In late 2007 and early 2008, Admiral was having trouble trading through 1100p. When the results came out on the 4th March 2008, you would have taken any profits, as they broke lower, despite the results being good.

See the chart opposite.

b) Take profits through a trailing stop-loss

Put simply, if the trade is moving in your favour, keep raising your stop-loss to a level that will lock in profits. (See chapter 5 for more on trailing stop-losses.)

Example

The buy or offer quote for the FTSE 100 June contract is 6000.

Original stop-loss level: 5900

A month later, the index rises to 6100

You move your stop-loss level to 6000

Two months later, the index rises to 6200

You raise the stop-loss level to 6100

Two and a half months later, the index retreats to 6100. This activates your stop-loss, but by this point you've locked in 100 points worth of profit.

---

c) Pre-determined exit points

Disciplined traders will set their **entry points** and **exit points** before they trade (and stick to them). These are really just stop-losses, but applied by the trader himself rather than by instructing the spread betting company.

d) Take profits due to technical data

There are numerous charting signals to show when a trend is reversing. See the charting section in chapter 6 for examples of websites on technical analysis.

When to cut your losses

Experienced traders understand that losing trades are part of the game. No matter how much research you do, no matter how carefully you check fundamental and technical data before placing a bet, no matter how confident you are about your decision, there will be times when the market moves against you.

The important thing is that on losing trades you keep the level of losses to a minimum and you do not allow losses to undermine your confidence.

As far as the first is concerned, you will find that cutting losses – in other words, closing a trade soon after it moves into a losing position – helps. Many traders, even experienced ones, find this difficult. The temptation is to hang in there, hoping that it will turn around. You must resist that impulse and pull out of the trade.

Another piece of wishful thinking is to assume that just because a share has dropped dramatically in price already, it is unlikely to fall further. Unfortunately this is not true. Shares often exhibit downward momentum as well as upward momentum, as people 'bail out of a sinking ship'. If you stay in a losing trade, be prepared to accompany it all the way to the bottom.

Examples

a) Due to fundamental data

> ### Example
>
> On September 1st, Peterhouse Group (an engineering company that refurbishes rail power supply in the UK) announced a 24% drop in income. The shares fell from 283p to 230p over the next two days, a drop of nearly 19%. Many investors thought that was the end of it, but shrewd investors who decided that things were not going to get any better decided to cut losses at 200p. On October 28th, the shares were trading at 119p.
>
> This is a good example of cutting losses even after a bad drop.
>
> The second danger posed by losing trades is that they damage your confidence, prompting you to doubt your trading strategy. But just because a trade went against you does not mean your reasoning was faulty, particularly if the loss was caused by a profit warning, a takeover bid or other unforeseeable circumstances. The critical thing is to cut your losses as soon as possible rather than keep the trade open in the hope that the trend will reverse. Chances are, you are exposing yourself to a bigger loss.

b) Due to technical data

Example

The chart below shows the price of £/$ or 'cable' when it broke through a major trend line. When cable broke the $2.02 level, it quickly ran down to $1.94. Stops would have been placed beneath the trend line to limit losses.

In chapter 6 we looked at support and resistance levels and how they can be used as the basis for buy and sell decisions. As a quick reminder, a support level is the price at which a share has, in the past, stopped falling; its floor if you like. A resistance level is the price which it never seems to rise above; its ceiling.

When you come to consider when to take a loss on a trade, the support level may be relevant. Imagine that you are long of Company X at 146p, and it has already fallen 3p to 143p. You might be wondering whether to take the loss or wait for it to bounce back. If you know from its share price chart that the company has never fallen below 143p in the past, that support level might encourage you to stay in the trade. If, on the other hand, its support level in the past has always been at the 135p level, you might reason that there is still plenty of downward movement to go, and it is time to cut your losses.

Key points

- Use a trailing stop-loss to lock in a certain level of profit but at the same time, keeping a bet open.

- Losing trades is part and parcel of spread betting. The key is to cut your losses early.

- The tell-tale sign of a beginner is that they take profits too soon and cut losses too late. Make a conscious effort to do the exact opposite.

10

It's a wrap

"To finish first, you must first finish."

– Rick Mears, Indy car driver

Closing an account

As long as all your outstanding profits/losses are settled, closing an account is the same as closing a bank account.

I want a refund! How to file a complaint

1. Tell your usual contact in the company. Complaints are usually resolved at this early stage.

2. If your contact cannot resolve the issue, the matter is investigated and they will contact you with the results of their findings.

3. If you are not satisfied with the solution, contact the company's compliance officer in writing.

4. If you are still unhappy with the result, call the Financial Ombudsman Service. This is an independent organisation set up to resolve disputes between consumers and financial firms. Note that the FOS will only investigate cases once your spread betting company has been given the opportunity to address your complaint.

   Their contact details are:

✉ Financial Ombudsman Service

   South Quay Plaza
   183 Marsh Wall
   London
   E14 9SR

☎ 020 7964 0500

💻 www.financial-ombudsman.org.uk

A final word...

Get rid of any illusions that the market will be kind to the meek, the slow or the naïve. It does not owe you a living. Once you place your trade, you are fair game.

After reading this book, the key is to put your new found knowledge into practice. Remember:

- Make use of the stop-loss at all times to minimise your potential losses. Preserve your capital.

- Have a game plan and stick to it.

- Accept that trading is all about probabilities. You win some, you lose some.

Learn. Have fun. Make money.

Resources

- www.advfn.com
- www.bigcharts.com
- www.bloomberg.com
- www.ft.com
- www.yahoo.co.uk/finance

Case studies: A tale of three traders

Sarah Mostyn: Brains over brawn

Sarah Mostyn* may have poured over books by Freud and Kant at university but today, she is more likely to be seen glued to Bloomberg TV and pouring over financial websites.

A 40 something year old home owner with a teenage daughter, Sarah discovered spread betting a year ago. She says: 'I've been trading shares on the internet before but I find that spread betting is more rewarding financially.'

Sarah uses her psychology degree to understand the market. She says: 'The market is also about human behaviour.'

She dipped her toe in spread betting in March 2003, after coming across a spread betting ad on the web. 'I compared the different spread betting sites and chose ETX Capital because their website was so simply presented and so easy to grasp.'

The main draw was ETX Capital's virtual trading platform. 'I did dummy trading for a month and started trading real money when I became relatively confident.'

The breakfast room in her Victorian house serves as her dealing room. While the smell of bacon and eggs in the air makes her trading headquarters a far cry from those in the City, her daily routine is not dissimilar.

She gets up at 7.30am and, still in her dressing gown, 'drinks in' the daily papers while sipping a cup of tea.

---

* Not her real name.

She says: 'I've got a Sky Digibox so Bloomberg TV would be on all day. The only time it's not on would be when my daughter's in and she switches it to MTV Base.'

Even then, Sarah would ask her to switch it back on to Bloomberg to check the prices during the ads.

Her trading schedule can be pretty sporadic. 'I would trade between 9.30am to 10.30am, the busiest times of the market. Then I'd go again at 1pm to 3pm, because that's when the market gets going. Then I'm busy again between 6pm to 8pm.'

Life wasn't rosy at the start – 'I made mistakes earlier on.' For example, one of her first punts was on the German stock market index DAX. While the DAX is ideal for short-term traders because of its volatility, it is not one that experts would recommend for novices. Sarah knows better now and mainly trades on the S&P: 'The DAX doesn't seem to follow a pattern whereas the S&P index, the FTSE index, the Dow Jones, they all follow a trend.'

In her first few weeks of online trading, Sarah learnt the ropes the traditional way: 'I would ring the spread betting company at least once a day for a couple of weeks. They were very good.'

One of her winning tactics was to open a buy position on an index, then when it drops down, she would actually add onto this losing position. 'The price rebounds back and when I see the profit, I'll take it.'

The method worked. 'By around the end of July to August, I was getting £700 a week. For two months, I did not have one losing trade.'

Sarah started to believe that her trading manoeuvres were foolproof. 'In August, I was really spending my wins, just going bananas. I couldn't see anything going wrong except the chance that someone would take my computer away.'

But her winning streak took a nasty turn at the start of September. 'When the dollar crashed, I panicked. I closed most of my positions and lost a lot of money, when in hindsight I didn't really have to lose that much.'

She says: 'I completely lost my confidence, and from then on every trade went wrong.'

Sarah considered backing out of the game altogether but her daughter persuaded her to change her mind. 'She said that I should keep going because it's something I love doing.'

After the bad run, Sarah clipped back her trading to twice a week. She adds: 'I'm not looking at trading shares right now, but when I do, I'd probably buy into AstraZeneca and one of the banks.'

Her advice to would be spread betters? 'You have to believe in yourself. I started failing when I lost my confidence.'

'Stop-losses can also work against you at times', she warns. 'It's trial and error. But I tend to choose the widest stop-loss level (the price furthest to the price you bought or sold at) so that I don't get stopped out unnecessarily when the market's volatile.'

To keep abreast with news, Sarah reads investment magazines, the newspapers and subscribes to several financial websites.

'But my Bloomberg TV's always on, that's my main source of news. I also spend much of the day looking at the charts, especially the S&P index,' she says.

Sarah believes there is the temptation to make trading unnecessarily complex. 'I think you can make it so much harder for yourself. I have a friend in Brighton who watches seven different screens. He ends up with information overload. The trick is to keep it simple.'

Patrick Gray: The man with a plan

It was 7.30pm on a cold Thursday night. While most people would have called it a day and were perhaps relaxing in front of the TV, a different scenario was unfolding in a lower ground seminar room at Bloomberg's headquarters in London.

In the middle of a room jam-packed with short-term trading neophytes sat Patrick Gray, a money broker at one of the largest derivatives and foreign exchanges in the country. He was there to learn more about buy and sell charting signals.

Like most of the audience, Patrick was a bit perplexed about how to interpret charts using 50% and 61.8% retracements or the overbalancing rule.

'It looks complicated,' he said, but he was determined to grasp the concepts. 'Statistics show that only one in ten traders actually make money. I want to be one of the 10% who do.'

Patrick started spread betting four years ago. His first punt was on Vodafone, a spread bet made after he spoke to a client who said there's money to be made on buying options in the stock. By coincidence, Patrick saw an advert from one of the spread betting companies and decided to open an account. 'I went long (buy) on Vodafone. I made a profit but I remember being very nervous. I think it was just £5 a point but it was quite nerve-racking because I hadn't done it before.'

He was also nervous because, while he was aware of the risk, he had no idea how to control it at the time. 'I could see the potential of it going wrong. But I didn't know about stop-losses then.' (A stop-loss is a way a spread better can cap his or her losses by determining, at the outset, when to close a bet if it goes against them.)

Patrick describes his foray into spread betting as a lunge into the unknown as he did not know anyone who did it. Part of the beauty of spread betting is being able to exit the bet whenever you want, a fact that he felt uncomfortable with at the start. He says: 'I didn't realise that I could go in and out of a trade without hurting anyone.'

'If I was to open a trade and close it the next day. I felt like I was mucking them [the spread betting company] around a bit. I thought it wasn't good to take up their time because if you book something for a three-month outlook and you take it out before that, I feel like I'm giving them extra work. I was completely naïve.'

Another misconception he had then was that he was betting against the spread betting company. 'I didn't know they were laying off their positions [the risks] in other ways.'

That was four years ago. Today, Patrick says he is much wiser and much better at his trades.

What are his tactics?

Patrick's normal trading day starts at 5.30am when he switches on Bloomberg TV to see how the markets in the Far East fared and the state of play of the major currencies. 'I look at the dollar against the yen and the euro against the pound.'

On the train ride to the city, he reads the *Financial Times*. 'Sometimes, there are interesting articles but most of the major news I already knew from the day before, as they were happening.'

As soon as he arrives in the dealing room, he turns on his computer and out flickers live prices of currencies, indices, the prices of the shares on his watch list and live Reuters news.

Patrick often bets on the German index DAX because the German market is open from 7am to 9pm. He reasons: 'Time is my biggest enemy. I would rather spend time with my family after work. They don't want me stuck in the study room at night.'

To get the punt right, he thinks working in the money market is an advantage. 'It's part of my job to look at the trading screens anyway.' He argues that the markets are interlinked and this means he can use his insight on the currency markets to play the stock market.

His success at the beginning of the year did go awry after he trumpeted his wins to some of his workmates who then gave him money to bet on whatever he was betting on.

The boast backfired.

'When I bet their money alongside mine. I started breaking my own rules. I wouldn't follow my stop-losses and sometimes, I would let my bets run longer than I normally would.'

What were the lessons learnt from that experience? 'Well, first, I'll always stick to my stop-losses and second, I won't get myself into the same position again.'

Ultimately, Patrick wants to spread bet full-time. 'I am trying to educate myself so I can do this as a sole source of income … I aim to make £1 million pounds a year, that would be my goal.'

Is he being too ambitious? Perhaps not. Patrick is pinning his future fortunes on a well-planned strategy rather than just luck. 'I don't do the lottery. I cannot see the point. I bought a property five years ago that has now doubled in price. I've got a pension and if I ever have time, I would manage it.'

While many think that spread betting is no more than glorified gambling, Patrick believes that unlike a punt on a horse, spread betting gives you more control of your losses and wins. If something goes against you, you can't just let it run hoping that it will turn around.

'You can't afford to have hope in this business, it just wouldn't work. If you hang on to the hope factor, you will get carted out.'

Alex Benjamin: Shaken but not stirred

Alex Benjamin's love affair with the stock market started in 1975, but the word 'love' is not one he'd choose. He made £60,000 in 12 months through spread betting by following one golden rule: You need to divorce your emotions from a trade.

Keeping a safe distance between his heart and his pocket is just one of Alex's trading tactics. Another maxim is that a trader must always have a game plan.

'The reality is that if you stand there without a game plan, you might as well write your bookmaker a cheque.'

With nearly three decades of trading experience under his belt – a passion that outlasted two (ex) wives and a combined payout of $1.2 million – Alex has collected a wealth of knowledge about the machinations of the City.

And so, as he speeds along the motorway en route to a black tie dinner in the Cotswolds, Alex switches his mobile phone to hands-free and parlays lessons learnt, pitfalls to avoid and the tricks of the trade.

For a start, learning how to trade is like trying to get a university degree. 'Trading successfully is not something you can achieve overnight or after three months,' he says.

'It takes a lawyer or a doctor seven years to get to where they are at. It's the same with being a trader.' In his case, he says, 'It could even take 15 years'.

Alex's worst trading lesson happened 20 years ago now, but the memory crashes back like it was yesterday. When the stock market suffered multiple heart seizures one day in October 1987, famously referred to as Black Monday, he sold all his shares in the ensuing months.

'I didn't realise that the October crash was a *one-day phenomena*. I spent the next six months selling all my shares and lost tens and tens of thousands.' In hindsight, he could have taken a deeper breath and bided his time.

For a man who is in the thick of the action on the bond, commodity and equity trading desks – specialising in arbitrage trading – it is curious to see him spread betting. Why is he interested in what is considered a more entry-level form of derivative trading?

'Very simple, you can trade in much smaller sizes and still get a massive exposure to the market. You know, it's about always trying to search for higher yield investments and spread betting is a form of that.'

With £1,000 initial capital and £1,000 credit from his chosen spread betting company, Alex started spread betting in the mid 1980s. However, a busy working life and day-to-day tasks got in the way and he stopped doing it for a while. He then picked it up when several spread betting companies joined the fray, giving prospective spread betters more choices and better spreads.

'Companies like ETX Capital have also benefited from being online.'

So how does he make money?

Alex's mantra is 'liquidity, liquidity, liquidity'. His trade of choice is the German Bund (Eurex) for this reason.

'You can go in and out very quickly,' he says. 'The spreads are very tight so it's often called "win or scratch" [win or cover your costs].'

Similarly, he also trades the S&P index. 'There is a tremendous amount of liquidity there too.'

One of his best trades in 2003 was on the S&P index. 'I shorted the S&P at 1030 and closed at 989.' Alex couldn't have timed his exit better. The lowest point that the index reached on that day was 988.

'I try not to chase the market, which is very much based on technical analysis. I'm an economist by background so I prefer looking at the fundamentals.'

That said, Alex uses charts as an aid to determine his entry and exit points.

His key tactic can be best described in one phrase: Stop or fruition.

'It's either you get the bet wrong and you close it at the stop-loss level or you take profits.'

According to ETX Capital, the average time a spread better holds onto a spread bet is five days. But to Alex, the length of time shouldn't be the main consideration.

'Before I do any trades, I want lots of my indicators going one way. The longest I've held onto a position is two years, and I got it right in the end.'

Trades do go wrong and traders should take that as part and parcel of trading.

'Look at how venture capitalists do it. They invest in ten businesses knowing that *nine* will go bust and that they will make money out of the *one* successful business.'

Engrossed in conversation, Alex misses his turn off the motorway and finally calls the dinner host to ask for directions. It's a bit of a metaphor for spread betting. After the call, he says: 'It's dark, I can't see the road signs. That's alright because I've got the map and the directions, I'll get there eventually.'

Appendices

Appendix 1: Comparison of conventional share trading versus spread betting

Conventional share trading (Vodafone Plc shares)	Spread betting (Vodafone December Future)
Shares trading at 122.75 – 123 (28th October)	Future trading at 123.2 – 124 (28th October)
Client buys 1,000 shares at 123	Client buys 10 pounds per point at 124
Contract Value = £1,230	Contract value = £1,240
Initial funds required = £1,230	Initial margin required = £124
Commissions charged = £10 Two months later (1% or £10 minimum)	No commission
Shares trading at 130 – 130.25 (16th December)	Future trading at 129.6 – 130.4 (16th December)
Client sells 1,000 shares at 130 point	Client sells 310 per point at 129.6
P/L* on trade = £70	P/L on trade = £56
Commissions = £20	Commissions = £0
Interest on cash = £0	Interest on cash = £6
Total P/L = £50	Total P/L = £62
ROI* = £50/£1,230 = 4%	ROI = £62/£124 = 50%

* P/L stands for Profit/Loss and ROI stands for Return on Investment.

Appendix 2: Spread betting at a glance

What is it?

A bet that the price of an index or a share will rise above or fall below a certain figure in the future. See chapter 1.

What are the pros and cons of spread betting?

Pros

+ Simple to understand and execute

+ Gains are tax-free

+ Stamp duty free

+ Can start with a small capital

Cons

− Deemed riskier than conventional share trading

− Possible to lose more than your initial deposit

− Losses on bets cannot be offset against capital gains from other investments

See chapter 1.

How do I get started?

Step 1: Read chapter 3 (Trading online – a step-by-step guide). A simple illustration is below.

Step 2: Practice your skills online using play money through a fantasy trading platform, such as on ⌨ www.ETXCapital.com. (See Appendix 3.)

Step 3: Start with a small capital. Spread bets can be made from an account balance as low as £50. (Real sample trades can be found throughout the book.)

Sections to read: The importance of a stop-loss (chapter 5), Spread betting strategies (chapter 8) and the case studies.

The bare bones of a spread bet:

Example: The FTSE index is trading at 5997. The quote from a spread betting company for the daily FTSE is 5996 – 5998.

1. You think the FTSE index will rise.

2. You place an 'up' bet that the FTSE will go up, and buy for 5998 at £1 per point movement.

3. You decide on a stop-loss level.

4. Scenario 1: You're right and the FTSE index rises to 6015 – 6017, you gain £17 (6015 – 5998).

5. Scenario 2: The FTSE index falls to 5988 – 5990, you lose £10 (5998 – 5988).

What are the key spread betting terms I should know about?

Read about stop-loss (chapter 5), margin requirements (chapter 2) and shorting (chapter 8).

Appendix 3: List of spread betting companies

Cantor Index

✉ One Churchill Place
Canary Wharf
London
E14 5RD
☎ 020 7894 8800
Fax 020 7894 8855
💻 www.cantorindex.co.uk
@ cs@cantorindex.co.uk

City Index

✉ Moorgate Hall
155 Moorgate
London
EC2M 6XB
☎ 0800 072 1107
Fax 020 7283 9619
💻 www.cityindex.co.uk
@ enquiries@cityindex.co.uk

CMC Markets

✉ 66 Prescot Street
London
E1 8HG
☎ 0800 0933 633
Fax 020 7170 8498
💻 www.cmcmarkets.co.uk
@ info@cmcmarkets.co.uk

ETXCapital.com

✉ Beaufort House
15 St. Botolph Street
London
EC3A 7QX

☎ 020 7422 3830

💻 www.ETXCapital.com

@ customerservice@ETXCapital.com

Financial Spreads Limited (part of City Index)

✉ Moorgate Hall
155 Moorgate
London
EC2M 6XB

☎ 0800 0969 620

💻 www.finspreads.com

@ enquiries@finspreads.com

IG Index

✉ Friars House
157-168 Blackfriars Road
London
SE1 8EZ

☎ 020 7896 0011

Fax 020 7896 0010

💻 www.igindex.co.uk

@ helpdesk@igindex.co.uk

Spreadex

✉ The ZigguratGrosvenor Road
St Albans
Hertfordshire
AL1 3AW

☎ 01727 895 000

💻 www.spreadex.com

@ info@spreadex.com

Appendix 4: Useful websites

Below are some of the more popular websites with useful information on spread betting or for market news.

- www.AboutSpreadBetting.co.uk
- www.ADVFN.com
- www.BigCharts.com
- www.Bloomberg.com
- www.BreakingViews.com
- www.CityHotDesk.co.uk
- www.CityWire.co.uk
- www.CQG.com
- www.DigitalLook.com
- www.EveryInvestor.co.uk
- www.Finspreads.com
- www.FT.com
- www.Fool.co.uk
- www.Global-Investor.com
- www.Hemscott.com
- www.MoneyAM.com
- www.Morningstar.co.uk
- www.Nasdaq.com
- www.Reuters.co.uk
- www.Sharecrazy.com
- www.Sharepages.com
- www.Sharescope.co.uk
- www.SpreadBettingCentral.co.uk
- www.Telegraph.co.uk
- www.TheBlindSquirrel.com

- www.ThisIsMoney.co.uk
- www.Tradestation.com
- www.Trade2Win.com
- www.Yahoo.co.uk

Trading software

Easysoft		www.easysoft-inds.co.za
Paritech		www.paritech.co.uk
Sharescope		www.sharescope.co.uk
Track Data		www.trackdata.co.uk
Updata		www.updata.co.uk

Glossary

A

Account limit

The total amount of deposit required from a client at any one time based on the size of the trade.

Arbitrage

The attempt to profit by exploiting the price difference for the same financial instrument from one spread betting company to that of another.

Auction

A system in which buyers and sellers enter competitive bids and offers simultaneously.

B

BACS (Bankers Automated Clearing System)

A system set by a group of banks and building societies to allow electronic transfer of funds to take place.

Bet size factor

The number used, multiplied by your stake size, to determine the margin required to do a particular trade. For example, if your stake size is £10 and the bet size factor is 10 then the margin required is £100.

Bid price

The price at which a stock, index or commodity can be sold.

Bond

A certificate of debt issued by a government or corporation that guarantees payment of the original investment plus interest by a specified future date.

Bookmaker

A company that will take on the opposite side of a bet that a client makes. A loose term to refer to a spread betting company. Usually, a spread betting company will hedge its client's bet by making a similar bet (see chapter 3).

Broker

A firm or person who, for a fee, acts as an intermediary (middleman) between a buyer and a seller.

Buy bet

A bet that the price of a particular financial instrument will rise. Also called an *up bet* or *going long*.

C

Capital gains tax (CGT)

Tax paid for profits made on an asset that has been held for a certain period of time.

Cash call

A demand from a spread betting company for extra funds to cover a bet that is losing money. Also called *margin call*.

CHAPS (Clearing House Automated Payment System)

A system in the UK to make cash payments in pounds. The receiver gets the fund on the same day.

Charts

Graphs that show the movement of a traded product. Chart patterns are used to make trading decisions. See *technical analysis*.

Closing trade

A second bet of equal size to the initial bet, but in the opposite direction and therefore taking a profit or loss. For example, a closing trade for a buy bet is a sell bet. Also called a *closing bet*.

Commodities

Physical products, such as foods or metals, which are processed and resold. Investors usually buy or sell these products through futures contracts.

Contract size

The smallest amount at which a futures or options product can be traded in. Also called a *lot size*.

Contracts for difference (CFDs)

A taxable derivative where the bid-offer price quoted is very similar to that of the underlying product. It is a type of margin trading because only a margin of 10-20% of the full cost of the trade is required at the outset.

Controlled risk bet

See *guaranteed stop-loss*.

Credit account

A type of account where the client does not need to deposit funds. However, proof that shows the client's assets are enough to cover margin and payments is required. The opposite of a *deposit account*.

Credit limit

The total losses a client with a credit account can run on open bets before it is necessary to send in extra funds (or before a *margin call*).

Currencies

Money in public circulation.

Cut and reverse

Closing an existing position and opening a new position through one trade. For example, you can buy 20 Dec Lloyds and sell 30 Dec Lloyds, resulting in a sell 10 Dec Lloyds. Also called *overclosure*.

D

Daily bets

See *intraday bets*.

Daily settlement

The official closing price for a particular market on a certain day. Also called *daily close*.

DAX

The index for the thirty largest stocks on the German Stock Exchange.

Deposit

The funds required as initial outlay for a bet. It is not the total amount that can be lost on a bet. Also called *margin*. (See chapter 5 on margin trading.)

Deposit account

An account that should have enough funds to allow a client to place a bet. The opposite of a *credit account*.

Derivative

A financial instrument that derives or takes its price from that of an underlying security such as an equity or commodity. The security themselves may not be needed for the trade to take place. Examples of derivatives are options, futures, contracts for difference (CFDs) and spread bets. Investors often trade derivatives to offset short-term falls in the value of the underlying security (see *hedge*).

Discount

The amount by which a price for one instrument is lower than that of a similar instrument. As opposed to a *premium*.

Dow Jones Industrial Average index (DJIA)

A price-weighted average of thirty actively traded blue-chip stocks on the US stock exchange, primarily industrials. The thirty stocks are chosen by the editors of the *Wall Street Journal* (which is published by Dow Jones & Company). This index is the most widely used indicator of the overall condition of the stock market.

Down bet

A bet that the price of a particular financial instrument will fall. Also referred to as a *sell* or *going short*.

E

Earnings

Revenues minus cost of sales, operating expenses and taxes, over a given period of time.

Earnings-per-share (EPS)

Total earnings divided by the company's number of shares. This number is used to calculate a company's price-to-earnings per share (P/E) ratio.

Economic indicators

Statistical data showing general trends in the economy.

Euronext.LIFFE

International derivatives business of Euronext, made up of the Amsterdam, Brussels, LIFFE, Lisbon and Paris derivatives markets.

Expiry date

The date a spread bet ends. The trade is settled automatically on this date unless the trader closes the bet beforehand or instructs the spread betting company to roll the bet over to the next expiry date.

F

Fast market

Terminology for a hive of activity. This is when prices change several times in seconds.

Fill

To execute an order. Used in the term 'fill or kill' which means you either execute a trade or cancel it.

FSA (Financial Services Authority)

The governing body that regulates the financial services industry, including spread betting.

FTSE 100

Index for the one hundred largest stocks on the London Stock Exchange.

Fundamental analysis

A method of judging a company's financials and operations. A company's fundamental data is directly related to the company's performance, as opposed to statistical data, which is used in *technical analysis*.

Futures contract

A legally binding arrangement where one party commits to buying an asset from another party on a specified date in the future, but at a price agreed previously. The counterparty is obliged to sell the asset at the agreed price and on the agreed date. Because the price is agreed at the outset, the seller (buyer) is protected from a fall (rise) in the price of the underlying asset in the intervening time period. Initially developed to protect agricultural producers from unforeseen market fluctuations.
(Source: London Stock Exchange, 💻 www.londonstockexchange.co.uk)

Futures price

The price that both parties of a futures contract agree to on settlement day.

G

Gaps through

Where the price of a certain security or market skips over the level you specified in a trade. A market either gaps up or gaps down. In a sell order, for example, if a market gaps down and does not hit your sell price, then your order to sell may not be activated. (See chapter 5 on guaranteed versus non-guaranteed stop-loss.)

Gearing

This refers to debt. A company's gearing ratio is its proportion of assets funded from borrowing relative to that funded by shareholders. A company with high gearing has a high level of debt in proportion to funds available from shareholders.

In spread betting, clients are gearing up because they only pay a margin of the total cost of their trade and the rest is effectively borrowed from the spread betting company.

Guaranteed order

See *guaranteed stop-loss*.

Guaranteed stop-loss

A stop-loss order that is guaranteed to be executed if the price hits that level or, more importantly, if the price gaps through that level. A non-guaranteed stop-loss is free of charge while a guaranteed stop-loss order is paid in the form of a wider spread.

H

Hang Seng Index

The index for the thirty-three largest companies on the Hong Kong Stock Exchange.

Hedge

A trade or an investment that reduces or eliminates the risk of loss from an adverse price movement in a position or security already held. For example, to compensate for possible short-term falls in the price of an existing share holding, an investor might short-sell the share through a derivative such as options or a spread bet.

I

Index

A statistical indicator that represents the total value of the stocks that it's constituted of. It often serves as a barometer for a given market or industry. It also acts as a benchmark against which financial or economic performance is measured.

Intraday bets

Bets that must be settled on the day they are made, unless they are rolled over to the next day or the next expiry date. Also called *daily bets*.

Investment-grade bond

A low-risk bond because the bond issuer has a good credit rating. The bond issuer is usually the government of a country, which is highly unlikely to default on the debt, such as the US or the UK. Due to the low risk involved, this bond has a low yield. As opposed to a *junk bond*.

J

Junk bond

A high-risk bond because the bond issuer has a poor credit rating (BB or lower) and therefore is more likely to default. Due to the risk involved, a junk bond usually has a high yield. As opposed to an *investment-grade bond*.

L

Leverage

The degree to which an investor or business uses borrowed money. In spread betting, traders are highly leveraged because they put up a margin on the trade and their spread bet firm effectively lends them the rest. See *gearing*.

LIBID (London Inter Bank Bid Rate)

The rate that one bank pays to another for a deposit.

LIBOR (London Inter Bank Offer Rate)

The rate that one bank charges to another for lending money. LIBOR is the lending rate for all major currencies up to one-year set at 11am each day by the British Bankers Association. It is also used as a benchmark for price derivatives and other market transactions.

LIFFE (London International Financial Futures and Options Exchange)

The three largest UK futures markets. Acquired by Euronext in 2001. See *Euronext.LIFFE*.

Limit order

An order to do a trade, either to buy or sell, when the price for the product you are interested in hits a certain price. A limit order is often placed when you want to do a trade but at a better price than the current quote.

Liquid/illiquid market

A liquid market has enough volume of two-way business for trading to occur without moving prices unduly. It will normally have narrow bid-offer spreads. An illiquid market normally does not have enough volume of two-way business for trading so a small amount of business results in disproportionate price movements. It will normally have wide bid-offer spreads.

Liquidity

The ability of an asset to be converted into cash quickly and without any price discount. In spread betting and share trading, it refers to how easy it is to trade a share. A stock's liquidity relies mainly on the number of shares available to the public (i.e. on free float) and the market capitalisation of the company.

Long

A position taken in anticipation of a falling market. To go long means to buy. As opposed to *short*.

Long bond

Another term for the US 20-year government bonds.

Long gilt

Another term for the UK 10-year government bonds.

Lot

See *contract size*.

LSE (London Stock Exchange)

The world's third largest stock exchange by market capitalisation of domestic stocks listed, after the New York Stock Exchange and Tokyo Stock Exchange. It is itself quoted on the Exchange.

M

Make up

See *settlement price*.

Margin call

In spread betting, this is the call from the spread betting company to a customer demanding the deposit of further funds to cover an adverse price movement.

Margin factor

See *bet size factor*.

Market hours

Normal opening hours for a market. Usually 8.00am to 4.30pm. Although some indices and shares may trade from 7am or until 5pm.

Minimum trade requirement

See *notional trading requirement*.

Momentum

The strength behind a price movement. Momentum investors look for upward or downward trends in stock prices or earnings. They believe that the price of a particular market will continue to head in the same direction on the premise that there are a large number of investors in the market who will buy whatever stock is already 'hot' or, conversely, sell.

N

NASDAQ Composite

An index of all stocks listed on the US Stock Exchange. This index is mainly used to track technology stocks and hence is not a good indicator of the whole market. See the *Dow Jones Industrial Average (DJIA)* index.

Nikkei

An index of 225 leading stocks traded on the Tokyo Stock Exchange.

Notional trading requirement (NTR)

The amount of available funds in your account that enable you to place a particular trade. Also called *margin required*.

O

Offer price

The price at which a stock, index or commodity can be bought.

Open positions

Trades that are currently running within a portfolio.

Option

The right, but not the obligation, to buy or sell an underlying financial instrument on or before a given date at the given price (called the *strike price*). A **call** is a right to buy while a **put** is a right to sell.

Order

A pending trade that is only executed as a trade when the trader's conditions are met. For example, a spread better might place an order to buy an index future if its price falls to a certain level.

Ordinary stop-loss

A pre-determined level at which a bet is closed to limit the loss on that bet if the price moves adversely. A risk management tool in spread betting. Also called *non-guaranteed stop-loss*. See *guaranteed stop-loss*.

Overclosure

See *cut and reverse*.

Over trading

Opening more positions then the account can support.

P

Pairs trading

The strategy of matching a long position with a short position in two shares in the same sector. This creates a hedge against the sector and the overall market that the two shares are in. (See chapter 8.)

Partial closing

Closing a portion of an open trade by making an opposite bet. This has the effect of locking in a profit or loss while leaving some of the original position open. For example, if you have an existing position of buy 10 Dec Lloyds and you sell 5 Dec Lloyds then you are left with an open position of buy 5 Dec Lloyds (half of your original trade). As opposed to *cut and reverse*.

Premium

The amount by which a price for one instrument is higher than that of a similar instrument. As opposed to *discount*.

Q

Quote

The price at which customers can buy or sell a particular index or share.

R

Range trading

A share or an index often trade within a certain price range. Range trading is about buying at the low end of the range (on the hope of a price rise to the high end of the range). Conversely, traders will sell at the high end of the range (on the hope of a price fall towards the low end of the range).

Recession

Defined as two consecutive quarters of negative economic growth as measured by a country's gross domestic product (GDP).

Return on capital employed (ROCE)

A ratio that shows the efficiency and profitability of a company's capital investments. Calculated as earnings before interest and tax (EBIT): (Capital employed + Short term borrowings – Intangible assets).

Risk

The possibility that the real return of an investment will be worse than expected. This could mean losing some, or all, of the original investment.

Roll over

To transfer a trade that is near its current expiry date to the next expiry date.

S

Screen price

The price of the underling security in the cash market. As opposed to *quote price*.

Sell bet

A bet that will be profitable for every tic that the price falls. Also called a *down bet* or *going short*.

Settlement price

The price at which a bet is closed.

Shorting

Refers to selling an asset you do not own with the aim of buying it back cheaper at a later date. In spread betting, it refers to placing a down bet or a trade in anticipation of a falling market. To go short means to sell.

Spot

The purchase and sale of a foreign currency or commodity for immediate delivery.

Spread trading

A term used in the US to refer to spread betting.

Stamp duty

A tax on foreign or share market transactions, usually a percentage of the total transaction amount.

Stop-loss

A pre-determined level at which a bet is closed to limit the loss on that bet if the price moves against you. See *guaranteed stop-loss*.

T

Technical analysis

A method of evaluating securities by analysing statistics generated by market activity, such as past prices and volume. Charts are often used as a tool to show patterns that can suggest future trends. As opposed to *fundamental analysis*.

Tick

The smallest possible movement (up or down) in the price of a security.

Trading resources

A combination of your cash balance, available credit, open profit or loss positions, and initial margin.

Trading tools

Aids to spot possible trends. Charts and market news are examples of trading tools.

TSE (Tokyo Stock Exchange)

The second largest stock exchange market in the world by market value.

U

Underlying instrument

In options, the security that must be delivered if a put or call option is exercised.

In equities, the common stock that underlies certain types of securities, such as warrants and convertible bonds.

Universal Stock Futures

Futures contracts on individual equities. These are traded on Euronext.LIFFE.

Up bet

A bet that will be profitable for every tic that a price rises. Also called a *buy* or *going long*. As opposed to a *down bet*.

V

Virtual trading

Some spread betting companies provide a virtual platform that mirrors their real money trading platforms. These virtual accounts are funded with 'play' money in order to give the client the opportunity to practice spread betting risk-free.

Volatility

A measure of the likelihood of a market or security to rise or fall sharply within a short period of time.

W

Wall Street

The street in New York where the NYSE New York Stock Exchange (NYSE) is located. Can also refer to the NYSE itself and all financial institutions in New York City, including stock exchanges, banks and commodity markets.

Wireless dealing

The opportunity to trade via equipment such as mobile phones and PDAs.

Y

Yield

The rate of return on an investment, usually expressed as an annual percentage rate.

In cases where a term has multiple meanings, this glossary will refer to the definition that applies to spread betting. Resources used to compile this list include the London Stock Exchange (www.londonstockexchange.com), InvestorWords.com (www.investorwords.com), TradIndex (www.tradindex.com) and other online, publicly available information from other spread betting companies.

Index

A

account
　closing 117
　funding of 21
　opening 25
　setting up 6
arbitrage 103

B

bet size factor 19-20
bid-offer spread 5, 8, 45-47
bid price 13
brokers consensus estimates 75-76
buy bet 16
buy stop 36

C

capital 5, 56, 92
capital gains tax 5, 8
case studies 119
charting 77
closing a bet 16
commission 5
complaints 117
contra bets 17
controlled risk spread 63
customer service 48

D

daily bets 26, 40, 47
dealing mechanisms 6
dealing rooms 27
derivatives 4
directors' dealings 74-75
dividends 5, 8
dividend yield 74
down bet 14

E

earnings per share (EPS) 70
economy 85
entry points 110
execution speed 6
exit points 110
expiry dates 8, 14, 16, 40

F

Fed Funds rate 85
Federal Open Market
Committee (FOMC) 85-87
fill or kill 36
Financial Ombudsman Service
117
Financial Times 85
forward p/e 71